BARBARIANS
LED BY
BILL GATES

JENNIFER EDSTROM
AND MARLIN ELLER

BARBARIANS
LED BY
BILL GATES

MICROSOFT FROM THE INSIDE:

HOW THE WORLD'S

RICHEST CORPORATION

WIELDS ITS POWER

HENRY HOLT AND COMPANY • NEW YORK

Henry Holt and Company, Inc.
Publishers since 1866
115 West 18th Street
New York, New York 10011

Henry Holt® is a registered
trademark of Henry Holt and Company, Inc.

Published in Canada by Fitzhenry & Whiteside Ltd.,
195 Allstate Parkway, Markham, Ontario L3R 4T8.

Library of Congress Cataloging-in-Publication Data

Edstrom, Jennifer.
Barbarians led by Bill Gates : how the world's richest corporation
wields its power / Jennifer Edstrom and Marlin Eller. — 1st Holt ed.
p.   cm.
Includes bibliographical references (p. 233) and index.
ISBN 0-8050-5754-4 (hb : alk. paper)
1. Microsoft Corporation.   2. Computer software industry—United States.
3. Gates, Bill, 1955– . I. Eller, Marlin. II. Title.
HD9696.63.U64M534   1998
338.7′610053′0973—dc21   98-12636
                                                                  CIP

Henry Holt books are available for special promotions and premiums.
For details contact: Director, Special Markets.

First Edition 1998

Designed by Victoria Hartman

Printed in the United States of America
All first editions are printed on acid-free paper. ∞

3   5   7   9   10   8   6   4   2

For Catlin, my soul mate

—J.E.

For Margaret and Eldon,

my parents

—M.E.

Actually, my only complaint is that I wish somebody had written a decent book. I just don't happen to like the ones that exist. They're incredibly inaccurate. Worse, they don't capture the excitement, the fun. What were the hard decisions? Why did things work out? Where was the luck? Where was the skill?

—*Bill Gates*

CONTENTS

· ·

ACKNOWLEDGMENTS

Hundreds of millions of copies of Microsoft software have been distributed across the planet, and it is a safe bet that you would not be holding this book if you were not already somewhat familiar with the company. My familiarity is of a different sort. I started as a programmer when Microsoft employed barely a hundred people. I stayed with it as a software developer and manager for the next thirteen years, as it evolved and grew to the point that it was hiring several people a day. When I left the company in 1995, it was about twenty thousand strong and still growing, its impact and influence continuing to expand.

During that time I watched the public perception of Microsoft go from ignorance—"Never heard of it"—to admiration of the fleet little upstart, and then on to fear and loathing of a seemingly unstoppable corporate juggernaut. As an insider, reading what the press and the analysts wrote over the years was a peculiar experience akin to hearing one's own voice recorded: "Is that really what I sound like? Is my voice really that gravelly?"

There was a great disconnect between the view from the inside that my compatriots and I were experiencing down in the trenches, and the outside view, which tended to be a stew of company-generated PR, promptly rejected by industry pundits as biased, only to be replaced with rumor and speculation.

While rumor and speculation have their own esthetic, my overall impression is that sound bites are too succinct and tidy, too neatly wrapped up—they miss the essentially chaotic nature of the enterprise. In their quest for causality they tend to attribute any success to a Machiavellian brilliance rather than to merely good fortune. They lend the impression that the captains of industry chart strategic courses, steering their tanker carefully and gracefully through the straits. The view from the inside more closely resembles whitewater rafting. "Oh my God! Huge rock dead ahead! Everyone to the left! NO, NO, the *other* left!!!"

This book is offered to provide some balance to that outside view. I do hope however that no one will mistake this report from the inside as an attempt at a balanced historical account, for indeed, items have been chosen primarily for contrast with the more commonly known perceptions of Microsoft. It is intended that the information contained herein will augment and temper your views of the company, help you see that reality is rarely a simple story and is probably more like a *Dilbert* cartoon. The life cycle of a thrashing beast with twenty thousand heads is not something that can be captured in any single document, including this one. *Caveat emptor.*

The production of a book such as this is the work of many hands. Many people have freely given of their time both in providing us with a wealth of material and insight and in helping us pare and trim it all down to fit in a single volume. The parade includes in no particular order or completeness our editors, parents, friends, co-workers at Microsoft, spouses, and immediate and extended families. There is not the slightest hope of naming them all, and rather than slight the majority who rightfully deserve praise and recognition, let me simply offer a collective thank-you.

And finally, dear reader, if you have made it this far, I would like to dedicate this book to you. If there had not been hundreds of millions of you out there willing to purchase our software, willing to play with it, to use it, to crash it and swear at it—sharing your time and your money and sharing with us both the wonders and the frustrations of this ongoing microcomputer revolution—then there would have been no Microsoft, there would have been no story and no audience. Truly you are the sunshine that has enabled this flower to bloom and grow, and I am deeply grateful to you. This has definitely been an E ticket.

Marlin Eller
Seattle, WA

I first met Marlin Eller back in 1994 while I was writing an article on video compression. Microsoft public relations arranged for me to interview Marlin, and shortly after, he said he wanted to write a book telling his inside story. The rest is history. The nature of the book has changed from its original concept of being a first-person autobiography of Marlin, but we decided to retain "Marlin Eller" as a central character as we shifted the narrative to the third person. This allowed us to incorporate both our voices as well as myriad interviews with others we would meet along the way. My utmost thanks go to Marlin, who gave me a great opportunity, put up with years of interviews, edits, and clarifications, and who also allowed me into his inner circle of fellow Microsoft veteran developers.

Like Marlin, I too am somewhat of a Microsoft insider, but in a different way. My mother joined Microsoft in 1982 to handle the company's public relations, and she continues to handle Microsoft PR from within her own agency, Waggener Edstrom. Since the age of thirteen, I grew up entrenched in Microsoft, personally watching Gates morph from the classic nerd to his now pop-icon status. But unlike Marlin, I never had the opportunity to get to know the developers, the guys who make Microsoft tick. Instead, I was exposed to

Microsoft's upper echelon of executives. I've been to countless Microsoft functions, ranging from wedding receptions to product launches to dinner with Gates. As you will see, the view from the trenches is refreshingly different.

Great thanks and appreciation go to all of the developers who took the time to share their stories—no holds barred—with me and to explain what it is really like to work at Microsoft.

Thanks to my mother, who always encouraged me to write—even if this wasn't particularly what she had in mind.

Thanks to Cheryl Currid, of Currid & Company, who provided much-needed inspiration, encouragement, and support throughout the project, and to Ted Julian for his analytical brilliance.

Thanks also to Bob Lorsch, and to Rowland Hanson, CRH & Associates, for the great color he provided and for his continual patience with the endless questioning.

Special thanks to Dr. Catherine Warren and Holly Hubbard Preston, for their excellent editing help and insights, and to John Domini, who helped in the early stages of the project.

Thanks to our agent, John Brockman, for his hard work, for taking on the book and finding us such a stellar editor and publisher.

And the highest of kudos to our editor, William Patrick, the master wordsmith of Henry Holt and Company, who took the reins and championed the book. Thank you for your time, enthusiasm, patience, guidance, support, sense of humor, and brilliant polishing of the book.

Jennifer Edstrom
Portland, OR

BARBARIANS
LED BY
BILL GATES

PROLOGUE

J im Clark smiled down benevolently at the spreadsheet. The fifty-two-year-old chairman and cofounder of Netscape Communications Corp. had just received the quarterly results from his chief financial officer. Fiscal year 1996 had not just been good. It had been great.

Leaning back in his chair, Clark focused on the sales figures. $346.2 million, up an astonishing 428 percent over 1995's results. An amazing feat for a company that had only been in existence since 1994. Certainly Wall Street was impressed. Since the company's initial public offering in August 1995, Netscape's stock had risen over 300 percent, finishing 1996 with a market value exceeding $5 billion. Clark's personal stake hovered around the $1 billion mark—not bad for a boy who'd grown up dirt poor in Texas.

The phone on Clark's desk rang. An operator announced it was time to begin the quarterly conference call. More than one hundred Wall Street analysts were awaiting a congratulatory chat with the chairman.

By this stage of the game, even Goldman Sachs, longtime advocate of Microsoft, had removed Gates's company from its recommended list and replaced it with Netscape. Analysts at the brokerage house said Netscape was the new leader in Internet technologies. Now Bill Gates and his teeming hoards were scurrying to play catch-up. They had to. After all, it was Gates who had told Wall Street analysts at a Microsoft briefing in December 1995, "An Internet browser is a trivial piece of software."

But by the time Jim Clark was ready to discuss his 1996 results with Wall Street, Americans had become accustomed to watching Pepsi ads with the company's Web address splashed across the bottom of the screen: www.pepsi.com. They were almost as accustomed to typing that address and a thousand others like it into Netscape's command line. Americans had logged on to the Internet with a vengeance, and Netscape dominated the Internet browser market with an estimated 83 percent market share. Microsoft was a distant second with a measly 8 percent.

Ironically, Microsoft could have owned that command line. But Microsoft had stared into the vast potential of the Internet . . . and blinked.

1

· ·

THE ROAD BEHIND

Microsoft, a rather new corporation, may not have matured to the position where it understands how it should act with respect to the public interest and the ethics of the marketplace.

—*U.S. District Judge Stanley Sporkin*

Nathan Myhrvold's pudgy fingers whirred across the keyboard as he peered into his 21-inch computer monitor. Most Microsoft developers would have killed for such a luxury, but Myhrvold was not just some hacker. He was a Ph.D. physicist who had worked on quantum field theories of gravitation with Stephen Hawking at Cambridge. He was also Gates's handpicked techno-visionary, chosen to lead Microsoft into the future. Myhrvold had always indulged himself with the newest and best—whether in technology or gourmet cuisine—even before his own company, DSR, was acquired by Microsoft in 1986.

He finished running a spell check through his latest interoffice memo, "Formats and Protocols for Consumer Information." Myhrvold typed blindingly fast. He had early on rejected the old-fashioned QWERTY keyboard developed to keep typewriter keys from sticking if people typed too fast. Instead he used the DVORAK keyboard, designed in 1936, which allowed him to type up to 100 percent faster.

And Myhrvold typed a lot.

The distribution list for this latest opus included the usual suspects: Bill Gates, Mike Maples, Paul Maritz, Charles Simonyi, along with key developers such as Marlin Eller and Murray Sargent. In total the memo would reach forty-four people, and it would change the direction of the company.

Leaving his secretary to disperse his literary output, Myhrvold walked into Eller's office. It was just two doors down from his in Building 9, one of the original structures that looked out over the fountain in the center of Microsoft's campus. Eller was a bright developer and also conceivably one of Microsoft's more stubborn ones. He had been there for years before Myhrvold arrived, and he maintained the healthy skepticism of an old-timer.

"Marlin, is your group fully staffed yet?" Myhrvold asked.

Eller looked up from his 17-inch screen and stopped typing.

"Ah, yeah," Eller said. "Thanks for sending Gordo."

Nathan grinned. Gordon Whitten was another bright old-timer and completely unmanageable, just like Eller. Myhrvold had decided they were the perfect match, hoping, maybe, that they'd cancel each other out.

Myhrvold turned and headed out the door.

"By the way," he said over his shoulder, "take a look at my memo. I've outlined everything your group is doing."

Eller rolled his eyes.

The memos Myhrvold wrote were internal sales pitches, mostly to convince Gates that the technologies Myhrvold talked about were worth funding. The memos were also territory markers, notifying other executives to stay off Myhrvold's turf. "This is what MY group is doing. WE will handle it." Included, also, were implicit warnings about any outside competition.

Myhrvold's memos often caused heated reactions among people at Microsoft. Developers like Eller gnashed their teeth over them because they included marching orders for technologies that were obviously decades into the future. And while some of Myhrvold's ideas were truly visionary, others were just plain bizarre. Myhrvold was a very broad thinker—he read a lot—but he was not necessarily a deep thinker. People who read Myhrvold's memos couldn't always discriminate between what was real and possible, and what was pure sci-fi. Myhrvold himself never appeared to worry much about that distinction, making his memos all the more dangerous because it was so hard to argue against them. How could you prove he was wrong when he was referring to something that might not happen for another ten years?

Eller had no reason to dread this particular memo. The research in his own group was going beautifully, and there was no reason to think Myhrvold's latest diktat would change that.

He left his office and walked down the corridor to the center of Building 9. All the buildings at Microsoft were shaped like an *X*. Supply rooms, mail rooms, and cafeterias were all in the center of the *X*. Microsoft had adopted the building design from IBM. This way the company could optimize the number of window offices.

Eller grabbed a Coke from the refrigerator, a freebie Microsoft provided for all its 11,000-plus employees, and headed for the mail room. He set down his drink and grabbed the pile of papers soon to be coming his way. On top was Myhrvold's memo. It looked thick.

Eller walked back to his office. The even thicker stack of papers on his desk seemed to have accreted since he left just a few minutes before. He much preferred the company's internal E-mail system. With E-mail he could just delete random messages and memos instead of filling up his in-basket and then his garbage can with slush. He spent two hours each morning pouring through hundreds of electronic messages, but as soon as 11:00 A.M. rolled around, he just pushed "delete." If the message was important enough, Eller assumed, the sender would try again.

He sat at his desk and glanced through Myhrvold's twelve-page report. The memo described the projects Myhrvold had in place to secure Microsoft's dominant position in the emerging market represented by the convergence of television and computers. Actually, it wasn't exactly Myhrvold's vision. It was a collection of other people's ideas brought together in coherent form. Myhrvold was simply the only one with the time to put the ideas on paper. Besides, he was one of the few Softies with a secretary to copy and distribute memos.

Eller tilted back his ever-present black beret and took a sip of Coke. Even in the summer he wore his trademark chapeau to keep his balding head out of the sun. In winter he wore a beard, in summer his smiling face shined through. He licked his finger and flipped to page four, which detailed the technology that Eller himself was working on.

Eller was in ACT, the advanced consumer technology group, which Myhrvold had recently set up. Gates had decided to make Microsoft the first software company with an internal division fully dedicated to advanced research. It would serve two purposes: to develop add-on products for Windows, and, as analysts have often speculated, to absorb some of the company's outrageously high profits, and thereby, ideally, lower the potential for further government scrutiny. Since 1988, prosecutors had kept Microsoft staked out as if they were the Gambino family, a trend that would only intensify as time went on.

ACT's initial effort was to focus on interactive television and other broadband network applications as well as low-bandwidth online services, a.k.a. Internet technologies. Myhrvold had several pet projects in place, the most realistic of which was the low-bandwidth Internet strategy, outlined in the memo.

Just a month earlier, Myhrvold had been standing with a marker at the white board, outlining different strategies.

"Low bandwidth is the way to make money now," Eller said.

Myhrvold scratched his beard and nodded in agreement. At least Eller *thought* Myhrvold's nod meant agreement.

The low-bandwidth idea was to connect computers together over the humble telephone line using standard protocols to exchange information in the on-line world. It was, in short, the World Wide Web. Of course, in 1992, the Web didn't exist at Microsoft or anywhere else.

Even so, the opportunity ripe for Microsoft at this moment was to create a standard protocol for the on-line world that everyone could adopt. Microsoft could then own the standards for all subsequent Internet applications—the Next Big Thing.

Gates should have been a natural at this. After all, he was the Standardization King. Before Gates arrived on the computer scene in the mid-1970s, a wide variety of different machines cohabitated, but none of them could communicate with one another, and they had little in common. Gates's first bolt of genius was to unify them with Microsoft's BASIC programming language.

Then, less than ten years later, Microsoft did it again. It brought graphics to the PC and set the new standard with Windows. So it was not a far-fetched idea that Microsoft could lay the same claim now to the Net. The Soft already had the knowledge to bring graphics on-line—Myhrvold said as much in his memo:

> I believe that we will see a replay of this situation. There will be dozens of crazy new consumer machines, each trying to do its own thing. Almost all of them will fail in the end, just as all early PCs failed. The ashes of these spirited attempts will be the incubator for a small number of standard platforms which will attain critical mass and ignite a mass market. Owning a standard on all of the candidates is an incredibly powerful thing because it makes it very unlikely indeed that you will be blind-sided by new developments. The trick for a software company in a time of hardware chaos is to make sure to have a bet placed on the eventual winners, and there is no better way to do

this in early stages than to have a way in which you can bet on all of them.

But Myhrvold did not spend the whole memo talking about low bandwidth or Internet standards. He and Gates were also excited about an evolutionary dead end called high bandwidth.

In 1992, Myhrvold was not the only futurist in the computer industry talking about the "grand convergence" of television and computers, a high-bandwidth strategy. Speculation ran rampant about a world with five hundred TV channels, video on demand, on-line shopping, and interactive games. Massive servers would house all of this information and shoot it down through fast wires into consumers' homes. It all sounded very intriguing. But also very far off in time. This was the *Jetson*-like world that captivated Bill Gates's geek imagination.

The emerging low-bandwidth Internet could have been a starting place for Microsoft to facilitate that kind of convergence, but low bandwidth simply didn't turn Gates on. It was too . . . mundane.

David F. Marquardt, a general partner of Technology Venture In-vestors in Menlo Park, California, and a Microsoft board member, recalled his amazement that Microsoft was putting so little into the Net. "They weren't in Silicon Valley. When you're here you feel it all around you," he told *Business Week* in July 1996. He brought up the topic of the Internet at a board meeting in April 1994. Mar-quardt described Gates's response this way: "His view was the In-ternet was free. There's no money to be made there. Why is that an interesting business?"

Gates instead would rhapsodize about a world with infinite channel choices, digital art on the walls, and computerized sound, light, and temperature controls throughout the home.

Ironically, these hubristic notions had already placed what could have been the key to success in Microsoft's hands. In early 1992, they had established a project called Homer to look at setting communications standards for the home. Gates would later use some of these ideas for his $53.4 million mansion on Lake Washington. And it was this initiative that eventually gave rise to the Remote Information Protocol.

The idea behind RIP, a concept that Netscape would later realize so beautifully, was to create a graphical user interface that would allow computer users to connect to information providers, much like today's World Wide Web. Microsoft already had an installed base of tens of millions of DOS and Windows users ready to go online. If Microsoft had simply bundled the RIP technology in the next version of its operating systems, the World Wide Web may have evolved in a very different way, leaving nothing for Netscape to create.

Myhrvold gave Eller funding and staffing for the Remote Information Protocol group, and Eller took a handful of people with him from the Homer project. In searching the company to fill the other positions, he wanted to make sure he avoided QVers—Microsoft argot for people who were "Quietly Vesting." Usually they didn't have more than six months before their stock options fully vested. Typically they were already worth a few million, so during their last six months, QVers weren't exactly motivated.

Microsoft was much more lenient about funding and forming groups in the early 1980s. In those days a developer would float an idea by Gates, and if it sounded reasonable, the money followed. Development leads were free to staff their groups with as many people as needed. The problem was, it was still hard to find enough truly first-rate minds to staff all of the groups.

The hiring policy for the company had always been an open call for bright developers. Microsoft had plenty of work available, so when a talented person was spotted, they were hired—they weren't necessarily hired for a specific position.

As standard Microsoft protocol, a dozen lead developers would interview each candidate, and of course everyone wanted the good ones. The head of the Excel group would decide they needed a certain developer. Someone from the Word group would claim they needed the person more. It became a shouting match.

Eventually, Eller emerged with about a dozen people for his group, most of them from within Microsoft. Some had just finished other projects in networking or applications, others were just tired of the groups they were in, and some had been in the old Homer group.

At this moment, Netscape didn't even exist. Sun Microsystems, a behemoth in the workstation market, was riding on hardware revenues from its UNIX business. They weren't focused on software—certainly they had not yet commercialized Java, Sun's now-dominant interpreted scripting language for the Internet.

So the Net just loomed there like a great white whale on the horizon, and Eller was finally in a position to build what he had always wanted—an interpreted object-oriented scripting language. It had to be lightweight, portable, and secure, just like Sun's Java is today. But the interpreted scripting language was only one part of the Remote Information Protocol. RIP encompassed a number of Internet technologies including a browser, like Netscape's Navigator, compression and decompression technologies, and encryption.

By December, Eller's group was rolling along. One day, Myhrvold caught Eller in the hall to discuss their progress.

"Hey," Myhrvold said. "I had this cool idea for doing image compression. Check this out."

Eller followed Myhrvold into his office. He sat on the leather couch while Myhrvold walked around the room waving his hands in the air, his eyes lit up, his voice giddy.

"You know that shaded computer graphics stuff we've been talking about. It occurs to me you could represent the shading by the electric field given off by an electron charge. Think about it— if you've got a collection of static electric charges, they create this electric field. It's more intense around the charges, and it falls off as you move away from the charges as an inverse square."

"Uhh, yeah," Eller said, pursing his lips.

"Well, but you see . . ." Myhrvold paused as he went to the white board and started drawing E and M equations. "There's all this machinery for solving electrostatic charge distribution problems, like Maxwell's equations. So you ought to be able to take a given electric field and figure out what the charge distribution would be to yield that particular field. Then you could compress the picture by solving for the electron charge distribution, and then just shipping down the locations of the electrons and what their charges are. Then the machine on the other end can reconstruct the picture by solving the field equation for the charges."

Eller scratched his head beneath the beret. It had been eighteen years since his college mathematics major. He didn't remember any of the equations for doing charge distribution on electrons, and he didn't want to look them up. It wouldn't have done any good anyway. Myhrvold was just throwing out some random and utterly convoluted way of doing the same thing Eller was already going after on a much more direct path.

Talking to Myhrvold was a little like smoking dope. It could give you "insights," but in the light of day those insights often didn't make any sense. Eller walked out of Myhrvold's office reeling and dizzy and looking for food.

How could Gates put this guy in such a powerful position? It's not that Myhrvold wasn't smart—he was exceedingly smart. But Myhrvold was a cosmologist. Cosmologists studied physics, but then they wandered off into the big bang and exploding stars and what happened in the first nanosecond. Among experimental physicists, cosmologists were known to be flakes. While physicists were rounding out to the thirteenth decimal, cosmologists were talking about wormholes and super strings and what happened before the universe began.

Plenty of developers resented Myhrvold. They were the ones who actually wrote code and knew the nitty-gritty. Myhrvold, being a big-picture guy, tended to forget how long it actually took to build something. Myhrvold argued that you could design a new graphics architecture in only two weeks. People like Eller, who had personally spent three years developing graphics for Windows, knew better.

Eller was still trying to regain his balance as he walked down the stairs to check on one of his people.

Everyone in Eller's group was in the same building, though spread apart. Microsoft's rapid growth had filled in all the nearby offices before his group had been fully staffed. Still, Eller worked hard to insulate his developers from upper-management politics, to allow them to focus on what they did best: code.

Ideally, Eller wanted to enable users to have a highly interactive—and very cool—user interface. He didn't want a huge server doing all of the processing work. If the server was doing it all, the server quickly became bogged down, and users lost their interactivity. The idea was to be able to take an application—a shopping form, for instance—download most of it to the user, or client, so that it was running on the PC, then let the user play with the form and customize it.

Eller had assigned a handful of people in his group to explore which interpreted scripting language they should use. Two people were looking at the C language, and one person was looking at transport layers, or how two computers would connect and communicate.

Two of Eller's people were working on hacking up Visual BASIC, and two others were working on the Forth language. The Forth language was originally invented by physicist Charles Moore in the late 1960s. It was a widely used, but little known, computer language, and it was very easy to port to different machines. It was tiny and fit in about 3 kilobytes of memory, versus today's systems, which require megabytes, a difference of five orders of magnitude.

Eller concluded that it was crucial to write an entirely new interpreted scripting language, and the issue was still a bit of a sore point with both Myhrvold and Gates.

"The last thing this company needs is another fucking language," Myhrvold had said.

Eller saw Myhrvold's mouth move, but when the cosmologist talked, it was Gates's voice that Eller heard. Gates wanted all of the languages to be the same—BASIC. After all, Gates had written it. But despite Chairman Bill's monument to code, the computer world needed to move on.

And Eller knew BASIC wouldn't work in this application anyway because the scripting language in RIP had to be compact and object oriented. So Eller's group forged ahead.

By the spring of 1993, the RIP group had made significant progress developing their lightweight interpreted scripting language. In fact, if they had stayed on track, they could have gotten RIP bundled into the then upcoming version of Windows 3.11, which was released in November 1993. What would Judge Penfield Jackson have made of *that*?

But things were already starting to disintegrate.

Myhrvold, who had earlier agreed with Eller that low bandwidth was the way to go, now seemed bored with the project. Instead, he was putting all his energy into the high-bandwidth interactive TV project.

Matters weren't helped any when, four months into the project, a buddy of Myhrvold's named Craig Mundie was brought in to be Eller's manager. Mundie, in his forties, had been the CEO of Alliant Computer—before the company went bankrupt. Alliant was a supercomputer shop that had focused on high bandwidth.

When Mundie came on board he promptly went to Eller's office to check on the RIP team's focus. This was December 1992, and he was not pleased to find Eller and his troops still working on low-bandwidth solutions.

"You're going to have so much bandwidth in the short term, it won't even be funny," Mundie told Eller. "Furthermore, wasting time on 9600 baud lines is just stupid. And last, but not least, you need to get with the program. You better get the message to your troops, 9600 baud is bullshit. You should be focusing on broadband!"

"Yeah, sure," Eller lied. "We can have a joint meeting, and I'll review the troops. No problem, Craig."

When Mundie came back a week later, he was surprised to find that Eller's troops hadn't got the message. They looked at Mundie with glazed eyes as he talked about how broadband was going to be all over the planet. They stared blankly as Mundie explained how people wouldn't need low bandwidth and that everything Eller's group was doing, squeezing bytes here and there to fit on a 9600 baud line, was just a waste of time.

Eller said nothing, and the entire group gazed back at Mundie with a placid look that, deep down, silently expressed, "Screw you."

Mundie followed Eller back to his office for a closed-door post-meeting and demanded to know why Eller's troops weren't on board.

"Well, you know, Craig, they're a hard bunch of guys, and they're kind of focused on the low-bandwidth strategy."

Eller paused for a moment, adjusting his grip for the proper spin. "And I don't know that we need to diffuse that thrust. I mean I'm sure that broadband is going to be great stuff in the future . . . and I'd be all over it if I weren't all over this project. But I am."

That's when it became apparent to Mundie that Eller was unmanageable.

Eller had been at Microsoft for more than a decade. He had spent three years in the "death march" to develop the Windows graphics subsystem, GDI, the graphics still used in Windows 95 today. He had also created Pen Windows, Gates's pet project at the time.

But as Microsoft grew, even top developers like Eller no longer had a direct line to Gates. In the early days of Windows 1.0, Eller had squabbled and sparred with Gates regularly. People on the Windows team had gone to movies together and worked till 2:00 A.M., happily hacking as the rock music blasted. Now there were vice-presidencies growing like kudzu. There were too many people to placate, to convince, to cajole.

Plowing through Microsoft's weed-infested org chart, Eller knew the only way to keep RIP alive was to take it straight to Bill.

A recruit party was coming up at the Seattle Museum of History and Industry, and Eller was responsible for chaperoning his newbies to the function. Recruit parties, according to a recent Gates memo, were no longer optional. This was a command performance.

Once upon a time, a recruit party consisted of a case of beer and pizzas in cardboard boxes. The developers would all sit in the lobby of the Northrup building talking to Gates about how great the world would be with their new software. But even now, with old-timers chumming up acne-faced kids over prawns and chardonnay, Eller still knew that, once the caterers started cleaning up, it would be an opportune time to talk to the boss.

After Eller's new hires had gone, he walked up to Gates in the "Keys to History" exhibit. The caterers were breaking down tables and chairs, and Gates was standing at the buffet chewing on a shrimp the size of Manhattan.

"Hey, Bill," Eller said.

Gates acknowledged Eller with a nod.

"I think we've got a good group here," Eller went on. "Especially that new kid who's gonna work with me on RIP."

Gates nodded again, but the richest man in America seemed otherwise engaged.

"You know," Eller said. "I don't think you're giving enough attention to low bandwidth."

Gates continued chewing, and Eller picked up a shrimp himself.

Gates looked at him and pushed the bridge of his glasses back up onto his nose.

"We have low bandwidth today," Eller continued. "Everybody has a modem. People can exchange information at 9600 baud. We don't need to wait for fiber. This way it's an evolution where everyone keeps their existing software and computers. We should do that now."

A long silence hung suspended between the two. Eller knew Gates had heard him. But Gates gazed off in the distance, seemingly oblivious to the Willits canoe, to the black and white stills of early Seattle settlers—and to Eller's point.

"Uh huh," Gates muttered.

And at that moment, Microsoft missed the technology boat. Millions of future Web surfers bearing the Microsoft logo simply turned and paddled back out to sea.

In the early days of pizza and beer, Gates would have been animatedly talking ideas with a developer. He would have been all over the issues, saying, "Why will this be more important than that? Is this really the right thing?"

Now Microsoft had become so big that Gates could no longer focus. Eller realized that Gates wasn't going to encourage anyone to support RIP. But Eller was tired of fighting, tired of persuading, tired of convincing. He walked away from the party disillusioned, but also realizing that maybe this moment of blindness was not really so unusual. Knee-jerk reactions and panic had always been a way of life at Microsoft. Working for Chairman Bill had been like white-water rafting, not ocean cruising. There were so many other near misses and episodes of dumb luck that the public and Microsoft investors never knew about. Now that the company had turned into its nemesis and become just another lumbering giant like IBM, Eller wondered how long market momentum would continue to carry it. Then again, Microsoft had three very substantial attributes to see it through: a lush array of laurels to rest on, enormous cash reserves, and a bone-crushing hold on the ultimate core asset—total control of the operating-system business.

If the past was any indication, Gates would be able to leverage that asset, wielding it like a club if need be, well into the future. And woe betide any competitor who got in his way.

2

. . . .

THE MAKING OF THE MICROSOFT

MARKETING MACHINE

> He had talents equal to business, and aspired
> no higher.
>
> —*Tacitus*

It was a Monday morning in Las Vegas, November 1982. The gamblers and working girls had all gone to bed, but on this particular day, as the desert sun cranked it up to "Broil," the usually deserted sidewalks along the Strip were teaming with thousands of conventioneers. Executive types, engineers, and home enthusiasts, the "computer people," as the local taxi drivers referred to them, were here for their annual pilgrimage to COMDEX, the largest computer trade show in America.

With identification tags hanging from their necks and large plastic bags of computer literature swinging from their arms, the COMDEX crowds marching up and down on their way to and from the Las Vegas Convention Center would never be mistaken for "high rollers." But among them, a twenty-seven-year-old en route to becoming the richest man in the world was scouring the vast trade show, looking for possible partners and competitors from within the hundreds of booths that dotted the floor.

When Bill Gates stopped at VisiCorp's booth he was struck like

Saul on the road to Damascus. On the computer screen before him, the old, artless DOS-based C:> prompt that Microsoft had standardized on IBM PCs was nowhere to be seen. In its place was a revolutionary graphical interface called VisiOn. With the use of a computer mouse, users could execute a series of commands by pulling down menus or clicking icons. It virtually wiped away the need for consumers to type in keyboard commands to move the cursor around the screen. With a user-friendly product like VisiOn, personal computing could make a major leap into the mainstream, and Gates knew it.

VisiCorp was one of Microsoft's stiffest rivals in the applications business, a market Gates was desperately trying to conquer. Now VisiCorp was encroaching on Gates's turf—operating systems—Microsoft's bread and butter DOS business. This was no minor threat.

VisiCorp, based in San Jose, California, had gained notoriety with a piece of accounting software called VisiCalc, an application that had propelled them into a $45 million dollar company—nearly twice the revenues of Microsoft. If VisiOn proved a success in the marketplace, VisiCorp would be positioned to set a revolutionary new computing standard for PC operating systems. Of course, *that* was the role Gates had staked out for his own company. Microsoft would set standards for the PC, not its competitors.

This could only mean one thing—and it was *not* a toga party.

After he saw VisiCorp's demonstration, Gates rushed back to Bellevue. He began canvassing Microsoft's in-house programming talent, seeking out the programmers best suited to duplicate VisiOn and exploit its attributes. Dan McCabe and Rao Remala, who had come to the United States in 1979 from an Indian village without so much as electricity, were his men. Since Gates had hired Remala, he had been socked away, working on Microsoft's BASIC (Beginner's All-Purpose Symbolic Instruction Code) programming language and its FORTRAN compiler.

Revenue generated by the sale of programming language products had been important to Microsoft since Gates and Microsoft's co-founder, Paul Allen, first licensed their version of BASIC to MITS (Micro Instrumentation and Telemetry Systems), the manufacturer of the Altair 8800, in February 1975. Programming languages such as BASIC, COBOL, FORTRAN, and PASCAL are high-level computer languages, resembling natural human language, which contain the specific commands that programmers use to build software. Once a program is written using a specific language it is then converted using a compiler program into numerical machine code, which are the instructions a specific computer can recognize.

Remala was tired of working on languages and was ready for a new challenge. Gates gave him one: develop a graphics-based windowing shell just like VisiOn, only better.

Remala and McCabe studied Xerox PARC's Star system, which Gates had purchased for Microsoft to reverse engineer. The $15,000 Star system had one of the most innovative interfaces available at the time. Icons of familiar objects like desktop folders, documents, and in-baskets decorated the screen.

The two developers spent the next several months writing code at a grueling pace. Remala was responsible for the window manager part, and McCabe did the graphics, a soon-to-be-controversial assignment vis-à-vis Apple's Macintosh.

Finally, by April 1983, the two had put together a prototype of a windowing system that mimicked VisiOn's. They called this new software the Interface Manager (IM).

At that point, little more existed of the product than its lofty name. Remala had created a demonstration showing overlapping windows that looked like sheets of paper stacked on top of each other—just how they would look on a desk. However, underneath those stacks of paper was nothing more than the set of instructions that put those graphics on the screen. It was a smoke and mirrors demonstration—not real working code.

Remala needed help, which came in the form of Steve Wood, a blunt, six-foot-two no-apologies programming legend from Yale. As a graduate student, he had been writing programming tools for minicomputers, then the dominant computing platform in the marketplace.

Wood was notorious for his elegant, meticulously clean code, which he wrote with blinding speed and accuracy. He also was fastidious to an extreme, so much so that when Kellogg's changed the color of the frosting on their raspberry Pop-Tarts from white to red, he dropped them, turning instead to Rice Krispy Treats.

Steve Ballmer, Gates's former dorm-mate at Harvard and now his number two, had heard of Wood from a fellow Microsoftie and began trying to recruit him in 1981.

"I don't want to work for a toy computer company," Wood told Ballmer. "I've got real iron here at Yale."

Microsoft wasn't the only company knocking on Wood's door. So was Xerox PARC, but Wood was even less interested in them. Never shy about pointing out the flaws he saw in systems, computer and otherwise, Wood saw the computer research lab as a pathetic place where great ideas for potential products died on the vine. Wood knew because he had spent a summer interning at PARC, at the end of which he gave a notorious speech to his fellow interns—and to his hosts—lambasting the place. Numerous PARC veterans shared Wood's opinion and had long since left the organization, taking their frustration and their ideas with them.

It wasn't until Wood married, in May 1983, that he began to reconsider Ballmer's offer to join Microsoft. It didn't hurt that Wood, a former Washington native, was also looking for a way to exit the joys of New Haven and move back to the Northwest.

Wood agreed to fly to Seattle to see what Microsoft had to offer. When Richard Brodie, a longtime Microsoft developer, interviewed him, Wood became annoyed, refusing to answer programming questions he thought were stupid; and told Brodie as much.

A man of no small ego himself, Brodie took offense, but Steve Ballmer was charmed by Wood's chutzpah and offered him a job.

On June 13, 1983, Wood joined Microsoft's flailing Interface Manager group. Immediately, he began to sense the chaos.

"We don't have a manager who cares about what we're doing," Wood told Remala. "We don't really have a clue as to what we're doing from a strategic standpoint."

The two programmers took their concerns to Ballmer.

"This is shitty," Wood said. "If you guys want to do something with a windowing package like VisiOn's, then you need somebody running the group who knows about it."

Wood wasn't bucking for the job for himself. He had no interest in managing anyone, much less a whole group. Furthermore, as Wood freely acknowledged, he had no experience dealing with windowing managers. Not many people did. His forte was writing software code for the kernel, the guts of a computer operating system that manages memory, files, and system resources, not the fancy graphical exterior.

About this time, Gates learned that Scott McGregor, the then twenty-six-year-old graphics guru from Xerox PARC who had written Xerox's windowing system, might be looking for another job.

Gates quickly flew down to Palo Alto to wine and dine McGregor. The two went to a Moroccan restaurant for dinner, and while the belly dancer entertained the other patrons, Gates went through his own very distinctive mating dance.

McGregor would later say that one of the things that impressed him most was not Gates's sense of rhythm, but his seemingly insatiable quest for knowledge. McGregor found that if he knew more than Gates on a particular topic, instead of being put off, Chairman Bill would obviously go out and bone up on the subject.

The next time McGregor saw his future boss Gates not only remembered verbatim their previous conversation, he proceeded to dazzle McGregor with his expert knowledge on topics that only a week before had stumped him.

McGregor headed up to Seattle to fly around in a helicopter, checking out property with his friend and budding helicopter pilot, and visionary software architect, Charles Simonyi.

McGregor, a dressed-down man who nonetheless maintained expensive tastes, liked what he saw of Washington real estate as well as what he saw of Microsoft. He took the job and bought a house that had once been featured in a design magazine. It was on Mercer Island, one of Seattle's more chic addresses.

Once McGregor came on board in the fall of 1983, Gates reorganized. He pulled the graphics groups away from Greg Whitten, one of Microsoft's earliest hires, and appointed McGregor to manage the new graphics project dubbed the "Interface Manager," which, much to the clamorous protests of developers, would later go under the name "Windows."

Marlin Eller, who had been working in Whitten's graphics group, joined Remala and Wood, rounding out the core of the Windows team.

Eller, a mathematician and former Williams College instructor, had been hired in 1982 to write a translator for Microsoft's BASIC programming language, but he quickly became sidetracked when he started playing with the boxy white IBM PC, introduced only a year earlier, and still a novelty at Microsoft. Like his cohorts, Eller couldn't resist the opportunity to jump on the keyboard and type in a few commands. The translator could wait.

Using a simple three-line piece of code, Eller drew a round digital clock up on the computer screen. It looked too plain. So he wrote some code that drew a colored yin-yang picture in the background. Using an instruction known as a flood-fill algorithm, he tried to fill in the background with color, but it didn't work.

Eller flipped through the manual, trying to figure out if he had done something wrong. He hadn't. He called his boss into his office.

"Why isn't the flood-fill working, Greg?"

"Must be a bug in your code, Marlin."

"No, I've already been over my code. There aren't any bugs."

"Not in *your* code," Whitten said. "In the BASIC code."

"Isn't this the BASIC we ship?"

"Yes."

"You mean we ship our BASIC with bugs in it?" Eller asked, somewhat incredulously.

"That's right." And with that, Whitten walked out of the room, effectively ending the conversation.

Apparently feeling he needed to further clarify the situation, Whitten appeared in Eller's office the next day.

What Eller had discovered, as Whitten explained it, was not a bug, but a feature.

Eller didn't buy Whitten's explanation. This was not a feature. This was a bug. In fact, this was bigger than a bug. A bug usually made the code perform a certain function that the programmer didn't anticipate, an unforeseen predicament. What Eller found was the great mambo design flaw. It prohibited the program from executing a command.

Slightly disgusted that he had just joined a company that was shipping defective software, Eller decided to take matters into his own hands. After researching graphics journals and spending nearly two weeks on this complicated problem, Eller finally hacked out a solution and wrote the new flood-fill algorithm. Though it was painfully slow and crawled across the screen, it did enable BASIC to correctly flood-fill.

Eller called his boss into his office once again.

Whitten was less than thrilled. He had authorized the work, but Eller had spent two weeks on the flood-fill, ignoring the translator he was supposed to be writing.

Undaunted, Eller set out to let others in on the flaw he had discovered and how he had fixed it. He pulled in any random developer he could find. He even pulled in Chairman Gates, whose office was just down the hall.

"Bill, check this out," Eller said, pointing to his computer screen. "I mean . . . who was the jerk who wrote this brain-dead piece of shit?"

Gates stared at the screen.

"See, now that's what I call a design flaw," Eller said. "Now check out my new version. Pretty cool, eh?"

Gates nodded, pushing his glasses up the bridge of his nose.

"Does it work with really complicated things?" Gates asked.

"Sure," Eller told him. He proceeded to draw a complicated object and flood-fill it.

"See? It works perfectly."

"Can you prove that this works all the time?"

"Uhh, well umm, kind of," Eller said. "I mean, I know it always works, but I'm a mathematician. The word 'prove' conjures up really ugly ideas."

Gates told Eller his program was nice, then turned and walked back to his office.

After Gates left, Whitten walked into Eller's office. He had heard the entire conversation.

"Do you know who wrote the original flood-fill algorithm?" he said, shaking his head.

"Ahhh, nope," Eller replied. "I don't believe I do."

Whitten paused, rubbed his finger on his left temple, and shook his head again.

"Bill wrote it," he said. "Bill was the *jerk* who wrote this *brain-dead piece of shit.*"

•　•　•

Eller would write GDI, the graphical device interface in Windows that sat on top of the kernel. Since graphics were essentially visual representations of math, Eller was perfect for the job.

As a kernel jockey, Steve Wood was responsible for writing the guts of Windows, the lowest level in an operating system.

Remala, already experienced with the Interface Manager demonstration, wrote User, the picture people actually saw on the screen and on their printers. User organized graphics into recognizable items like icons, menus, dialog buttons, and scroll bars and gave Windows its look and feel, which, of course, bore a striking resemblance to the Apple Macintosh, a similarity that would lead in time to Apple's 1988 copyright infringement suit against Microsoft.

McGregor and his team gathered in the conference room to discuss what exactly it was they were going to build. Their only guidance from Gates was to squash VisiOn. As for technical direction, the Windows team was left to their own devices.

The entire ambition for the Windows team was to create something "cool" that was also visually stimulating to the eye. Their goal was to create a virtual software layer that would unite the hardware and software marketplace on a single standard—a standard, once again, controlled by Microsoft. They wanted developers writing applications for Windows that would then run on any hardware. Likewise, hardware vendors who supported Windows could run all the software on the market. Then Microsoft could charge royalties to the hardware vendors and also make money writing its own software for the system. The potential for revenues was huge.

But the challenges were enormous.

For every piece of hardware and software on the market, Microsoft would have to write drivers, little chunks of code that let the computer know what it was running.

In 1983, the Windows group had fewer than ten people. It would be impossible for the team to write all of the drivers themselves, especially given their tight deadline, which was just months away. What they had to do was convince the hardware and software vendors to do the work for them.

Even though the Windows team was far from achieving its goal of an operating system–driven, graphical user interface, they had to have Windows endorsements from the hardware and software development communities. If there weren't any applications available for Windows, nobody would buy the platform. Similarly, if the applications didn't exist, hardware vendors wouldn't support Windows by putting it on their machines. Chicken and egg, hardware and software.

Microsoft had to convince the hardware vendors of this: "The world is moving to graphics. If you don't write drivers for Windows, you'll miss the boat! In the future, all applications will be written for Windows, and no one will write to your hardware."

At the same time, Microsoft had to convince the software developers that all of the hardware manufacturers were building drivers for Windows.

Microsoft started with the software developers, saying, "You don't want to write drivers for hundreds of devices, do you?"

Next, they worked over the hardware manufacturers. "Look at all the developers we've signed up who have agreed to write all of their future software for Windows. You'd better write drivers for Windows, or none of their applications will run on your hardware."

Then, they went back to the software developers and repeated the drill.

Gates and McGregor went on several trips together, trying to convince both the hardware and software makers to jump on the Windows bandwagon. They always flew coach and often took red eyes, and McGregor was taken aback by Gates's and Microsoft's hardball methods.

Asked to describe the process years later, McGregor remembered it this way: "Bill would go to a very senior person at these other OEMs whether it was DEC or Tandy or Compaq or whoever and yell at them or tell them it had to be this way, or if you don't do this we'll make sure our software doesn't run on your box," McGregor said. "What do you do if you're one of these OEM guys? You're screwed. You can't have Microsoft not support your hardware so you better do what they say."

Ironically, McGregor also remembered the remarkable transformation of William Gates III in front of IBM. "Bill was very humble and would speak softer [with IBM]. There was a definite difference in the tone of his voice," McGregor said. "You'd go in the meeting and it was just a fascinating contrast to see Bill at IBM versus Bill at any of the other companies." He would even wear a suit and tie.

• • •

In late 1982, not long after he ordered his troops to copy VisiOn, Gates embarked on creating what would become Microsoft's most marketable product: its image. Until this point, like most other companies in the fledgling PC industry, Microsoft had relied on the computer trade press, as well as word of mouth, to market its products. These efforts, while successful among the technical elite, did little to capture the attention of the broader, consumer-mainstream.

In the fall of 1982, Pam Edstrom, a diminutive woman with piercing blue eyes, was recruited by Microsoft. Edstrom had been working at Tektronix, a high-technology electronics instrumentation company in Beaverton, Oregon, but when Jim Towne, Tek's general manager, was hired by Microsoft to become the company's first president, Edstrom quickly followed. Edstrom was driven, not just by ambition but by the very real need to put food on the table. This motivation helped turn her into one of the most aggressive, calculating, successful public-relations executives in the country.

Even though she was, at thirty-six, one of the oldest employees at Microsoft, Edstrom would have to work hard to earn the respect of her fellow employees, the then mostly male programmers. In their eyes she was a "flack," a term that originated with the flak jackets pilots wore in World War II to protect against shrapnel. In modern-day business, flacks were responsible not only for avoiding bad press, but for spinning the good. Edstrom was not just a flack, she was a brilliant strategist. She would help take industry marketing to a whole new, and not always fair, level.

In the eyes of Microsoft's jaded programmers, Edstrom and her breed were a necessary evil to be tolerated at best. What they couldn't know at the time was that Edstrom, along with a few other key hires on the marketing side, were about to change not just the face, but the soul of Microsoft forever.

Not long after Edstrom signed on, she was joined by Rowland Hanson, the former vice president of marketing for Neutrogena Corporation, a maker of soap and cosmetics. Good looking, well dressed, and a computer virgin, Hanson, a die-hard surfer and beach lover, came from a world of fragrant packaged goods where appearances—image and perception—were everything. He represented all that Microsoft, in the early 1980s, was not.

Until 1983, the computer industry was still so arrogant that it had no idea how truly bush league it was when it came to packaging and pitching products for consumers. Gates, in the early 1980s, was the epitome of this clueless arrogance, but he and Microsoft were about to receive a face-lift.

Hanson and Edstrom would spin a whole new image for Gates himself. They would tap the best and worst of Chairman Bill, changing his clothes, his voice, and his allegiances, driving him to become not just the boss, but, essentially, the company mascot—a sort of high-technology Colonel Sanders.

Hanson, who always longed to own his own business, had been getting ready to leave Neutrogena and launch a new line of pet care products. Just before getting the seed money he needed for his new venture, he took a call from a New York–based search firm responsible for recruiting executives for Microsoft.

"Here's the type of guy I want," Gates told the headhunters. "I don't care if he knows anything about computers. I need a guy who really understands branding."

If Hanson could create market differentiation for something as straightforward as hand lotion, Gates reasoned, then why not do the same with software?

Hanson didn't fancy himself much in the nerdy world of computers, nor was he eager to trade in southern California sunshine for rain. But as a favor to the headhunter, or merely to get him off his back, Hanson agreed to fly up on a Sunday morning to meet with Gates.

Hanson got on the plane to Seattle with every intention of saying no. Microsoft's Steve Ballmer, Gates's dorm-mate at college and now chief confidant, who had earlier spent a brief stint at consumer-goods giant Proctor & Gamble, picked up Hanson at the airport, and the two hit it off immediately, talking football on the drive to Bellevue. A husky six-feet-one, two hundred twenty-five pounds, Ballmer had once been student manager of the Harvard football team.

When they got to Gates's office, the young chairman immediately launched into sales mode, rocking back and forth with excitement as he explained his vision of computing.

It was all Greek to Hanson, but then a light went off in his head. In Microsoft he saw a "marketing" Pygmalion . . . with Gates as Eliza Doolittle.

"I'm starting to get what you're talking about here," Hanson said. He was fascinated with the birth of new industries, a soldier of fortune always looking for a new marketing challenge. "But I have no idea why you're interested in me. I don't know anything about computers, I don't own one. I know nothing about software. Why are you even talking to me?"

Gates looked puzzled. "I thought you understood," he said.

Hanson shook his head.

"What's the difference between a dollar-per-ounce moisturizer and hundred-dollar-an-ounce moisturizer?"

"Technically . . . there is no difference. Vaseline works as well as Clinique's daily moisturizer. It may even be more effective."

"So what's the difference?" Gates asked.

"Well, it's in the brand. The image you create around the brand."

"That's why I need you in this company," Gates said. "Because nobody in this company, or in this industry, really understands that. And if we can have the perception, I can create the reality. With the combination of the reality and the perception, nobody will ever beat us."

Hanson was sold. But it would take three months of negotiating to bring him to Microsoft. One of the stipulations, Hanson said, was that he would only stay at Microsoft for a couple of years. After that, he would start his own business.

Sure, Gates agreed, confident that Hanson Pet Care Products would never see the light of day.

Hanson joined Microsoft in early 1983. As vice president of corporate communications, Hanson was responsible for advertising, public relations, and anything having to do with retail promotions and the public. Hanson's goal was to position the company as the industry leader in software. But to get there, they would need to establish certain fundamentals.

Microsoft was an environment in transition—sort of like Beirut is in transition—a company with no checks and balances, dominated entirely by developers. They did what they wanted, when they wanted. Procedures didn't exist. Hanson liked the challenge.

Hanson's goal was to position Microsoft as the "safe buy, the quality buy," i.e., the next IBM. Hanson not only began changing what Microsoft said, he began a makeover in how the company appeared to corporate America. If Microsoft wanted to be the "safe buy," people had to see Microsoft the same way they saw IBM—stable, hardworking, straight up and down.

IBM didn't always make the best hardware—its PC Junior machine had been a disaster and eventually people would realize that. But for a long time, people bought IBM because of the perception of safety. Nobody purchasing computers in corporate America was going to stick his neck out by buying some jerk-off brand. You had to buy a brand you could defend to your nontechnical senior management, as well as to shareholders. Gates knew that victory meant people simply asking for the Microsoft brand.

But if Hanson was going to position Microsoft in a certain way, he first had to understand what people thought about the company. He proposed spending $50,000 on the first awareness and attitude study in the computer industry. He knew of a company called Griggs and Anderson, a Portland, Oregon–based research house, that had been doing focus groups. The research would evaluate not only the general awareness and perceptions of Microsoft, but also what features Microsoft should be including in its products.

Gates's reaction to Hanson's plan was: "This is insane."

He and Hanson battled back and forth. Then at one of their Monday-morning strategy meetings with Microsoft's other top executives the bickering came to a head.

"We're not going to do it," Gates shouted.

Hanson pressed on. "I need to proceed with this research," he said. "We're not going to get it done in time, and I have ad schedules to make. A lot of this is going to be used."

Right then in front of everybody, Gates reversed his position.

"You're right," Gates said. "Let's do it."

"That's why Gates was so successful," Hanson would later reflect. "His ability to turn on a dime, and to listen to the smart people he surrounded himself with."

The next item on Hanson's agenda was to figure out the message Microsoft wanted to deliver.

Griggs and Anderson performed their focus groups, comparing Microsoft with other companies such as VisiCorp and IBM.

The survey results provided some pretty compelling, if not damning evidence. People said they wouldn't purchase Microsoft's software because they couldn't understand the packaging—pure techno-babble. People were also turned off by Microsoft's own forest green logo, dubbed the "Blibbet," that had the name Microsoft, with the letter O crisscrossed with horizontal lines, which to this day has defied interpretation.

The results told Hanson how people viewed each company and exactly what it would take for people to perceive Microsoft as the industry leader. He took that input and developed the necessary message. It was a very disciplined, systematic approach—something totally alien to the boys' club of techies who relished their *Animal House* ways.

Hanson and his team knew the company had to have a sole spokesman to make sure the message to the public remained controlled and focused. Before Hanson arrived on the scene, the absence of formal Microsoft marketing procedures left developers calling the shots. They chose the awful names and wrote the impenetrable lingo on the back of the boxes. They talked freely to the press, improvising randomly, trying to evangelize the company, but instead spreading inconsistency and wild incoherence.

In Hanson and Edstrom's view of the world, Gates should be Microsoft's spokesman. Microsoft's cofounder, Paul Allen, had resigned in 1983 after battling Hodgkin's disease, and Gates fit the consummate developer image.

Hanson sent around a gag order—no talking to the media. This was, to say the least, not a popular decision with Microsoft's developers.

Developers were also skeptical about Hanson's decision to change the manuals and the packaging based on consumer feedback. Some developers thought if the consumer was too stupid to understand the manual, they probably shouldn't be using the product in the first place.

Hanson ignored this arrogance. For him and for Microsoft, the Griggs and Anderson research was proving invaluable. As their study showed, other leading companies had the same problem of consumers not making the association between a company and its products. Almost everyone knew the premier word processor at the time, WordStar, yet no one knew that MicroPro made the software.

The company never appeared on the radar screen. Likewise, consumers participating in the study knew dBASE, the predominant database product, but no one had ever heard of its maker, Ashton-Tate.

The key to Hanson's and Microsoft's success was to have a naming strategy for Microsoft products, and for the company to enforce the brand. Instead of "Word" as a word processor, it would be called "Microsoft Word." Multiplan, Microsoft's spreadsheet, would be called "Microsoft Excel."

Hanson knew that products and product versions would come and go, but that the Microsoft brand name would live on. Microsoft—and Bill Gates—would be the heroes.

Not everyone shared Hanson's affection for brand awareness. In fact, he ran into an uproar with the developers. Naming strategies, branding strategies, whatever those were—the developers didn't know and didn't care. It all sounded like grandiose flackery to them.

The developers, as a whole, still wanted to call their new windowing system the Interface Manager. That was a name they had come up with and it was the flag they were carrying. In the developers minds, this was *their* product. They had built it—not Hanson.

But from a marketing standpoint the name sucked, big time, and that's all Hanson cared about.

Knowing they wanted to keep Microsoft as the hero, Hanson, Edstrom, and the corporate communications team began brainstorming new names for I.M. No one, including Hanson, understood what a windowing environment was. There were different products from companies like VisiCorp, and they all had hip names, like "VisiOn," but the names had nothing to do with the product itself.

To sort through the confusion, Hanson took all of the editorial clips and news stories on these windowing systems and looked to see what they had in common. Consistently, the press was calling this new thing a windowing shell, a windowing manager, or a windowing system. If Microsoft wanted to set a de facto standard in the industry, the logical generic name to call the new product was "Windows."

The developers held on to Interface Manager. Gates didn't want to get involved. He insisted that Hanson convince the others that the name should be Windows. But Hanson was stonewalled.

To the developers, Hanson was the "cosmetics guy," the guy who knew nothing about computers or software and sure as hell wasn't in a position to name their product.

Frustrated, Hanson went back to Gates.

"I've given everybody the logic on this and nobody is buying it," he said. "You have to make the decision. I can't convince them. We've got a naming strategy, which is based on our branding strategy. Our branding strategy is based on how we want to position Microsoft. Now we've got this 'thing' that fits within our naming strategy, and the only logical thing to call it, if we believe in all this crap we've been talking about, is 'Windows.' There is no other name."

Just before the Windows documentation was to be printed, Gates the oracle spoke. Then the developers lined up behind him with their support.

So now they had a name, but Hanson and Edstrom still weren't sure whether Microsoft was ready to make an announcement. A technical neophyte, Hanson had no idea what was realistic timing on the product side. In his experience in the food and cosmetics industries, when someone promised a product would be delivered on a particular date, the schedule was simply a function of safety testing. It was guaranteed. Hanson's job was never to question the date, but to line up behind it and salute.

Edstrom, coming out of Tektronix, was technically more savvy, and she provided Hanson with wisdom born of experience. Hanson would walk out of a meeting with developers thinking everything was "golden." Edstrom would look at Hanson and shake her head.

"Big problem," she'd explain. "This stuff isn't going to be ready."

Hanson remained unconcerned. From a communications stand-point, everything seemed to be in order. But Edstrom knew better. Sure, she told him, if *nothing* went wrong, if there were no bugs in the software, if the gods smiled, if the Red Sox won the World Series . . . the developers might just make the date. But in the software industry . . . dream on.

Gates, who should have known better, gave the go-ahead for Windows's launch, and he sanctioned not one, but two announcements, a spectacular coming-out party for Microsoft as well as for Windows.

The first would take place on November 10, in New York. Microsoft had successfully romanced twenty-four different computer manufacturers who would publicly pledge their support for Windows. Noticeably absent, however, was IBM. Big Blue didn't care about graphics, and it wasn't buying Windows.

Despite IBM's wariness, Microsoft was able to show that Windows would run on a slew of different machines. The beautiful part of the New York event was the twenty-four original equipment manufacturers, OEMs, which Microsoft had recruited to the Windows bandwagon, assembled on stage together. Many of these companies were blood rivals who normally wouldn't be within spitting distance of each other. Yet Microsoft, in the name of what must be one helluva new product, was able to pull them all together.

As Edstrom, Hanson, and Gates saw it, this was the shape of things to come—Microsoft writ large, Microsoft *über alles.*

The second phase—the pièce de résistance—would be Las Vegas, the computer industry's biggest trade show, COMDEX.

• • •

Begun in 1979, COMDEX, the computer distributors' exhibition, had become *the* scene, where industry go-getters had to be, and where opinion makers and trendsetters gathered in full force to see and be seen. By 1983, it was a huge phenomenon, and with all that ballyhoo, it was very difficult for any company, much less a small upstart like Microsoft, to be noticed at all.

Once Hanson knew that Microsoft would launch Windows at COMDEX, the entire communications department embarked on a mad frenzy. Gates had made it perfectly clear that the launch of Windows was the Super Bowl, and Gates didn't just want to play . . . he wanted to *win*. Knowing that, Hanson's goal was two-fold: to make Windows a phenomenon, and to create *the* buzz in the industry with Microsoft. Immediately, they faced huge obstacles.

For starters, all of Las Vegas was booked solid.

Hanson called Bob Lorsch, a marketing mastermind, with a Los Angeles–based sales promotion agency whom Hanson had used in crisis mode at Neutrogena.

Hanson said, "I need to own Las Vegas during this event. I don't care what the rules are. We need to rise above the clutter."

Then Hanson warned his team. "We're never going to get this done working through the normal channels. The normal channels are all taken. I mean this is an insane launch plan. I need to bring in somebody who can make the impossible happen. And you need to trust me. This guy is going to scare you because he is a little bit off the wall."

When people showed up in Las Vegas, they were awestruck. There wasn't a taxi on the Strip not promoting Windows. Stickers were all over the backseats of cabs; the drivers wore Windows buttons.

These same buttons were handed out at the booths of every hardware manufacturer that supported Windows. Each button had a number on it. If people could find someone else with a number that matched theirs, they could go to the Microsoft booth together and receive software, gifts, and a bombast of Windows hype. In a Disneyesque mode, Lorsch also created wuppies—little fuzzy mice holding Windows flags—to promote Microsoft's new mouse.

Lorsch was a magician who believed anything was possible and simply wouldn't take no for an answer. He managed to get Windows 1.0 pillowcases placed in 20,000 Las Vegas hotel rooms. When half-asleep COMDEX attendees turned down their beds at night, they were astonished to find their pillows instructing them to stop by Microsoft's booth. Windows 1.0 marketing materials were subversively slipped under hotel doors. Every day, during the entire week of COMDEX, Microsoft had new and different promotional materials delivered to the hotel rooms.

Microsoft's competitors were crazed, but Gates and his marketing crew were ecstatic. People couldn't go to bed without Windows. Microsoft had a huge Windows sign right outside the front lobby of the Las Vegas Convention Center. Microsoft was dancing in the end zone.

As for Hanson himself, he was accustomed to trade shows in Las Vegas, but not to computer conventions. He was used to walking down the Strip talking to beauty editors and fashion models from *Vogue* and *Vanity Fair*. Now he was staring at programmers with plastic pocket protectors.

Microsoft's colossal cocktail party at Caesar's Palace—suits and ties were the order of the day—brought Hanson somewhat closer to his own element. Naturally, it was Hanson who had demanded that the Windows developers show up for the party looking like IBMers, or not show up at all.

Only a handful of the Windows 1.0 developers toed the line. Most boycotted the party to protest the dress code—many didn't even *own* a suit. Still, it was a roaring success.

Microsoft arranged for country singer Glen Campbell to show up for the soiree and give a speech. Dressed in cowboy boots, the "Rhinestone Cowboy" stood incongruously next to the world's soon-to-be-most-famous computer geek.

"I just wanted to welcome y'all here for the Microsoft party," Campbell said in his Arkansas drawl. "And I just want to let you know this is my good buddy Bill Gates."

The crowd laughed till it hurt.

But the buzz was no joke. Because of this Hanson-inspired blitz, Microsoft went from being a player to being *the* player. Nobody had ever owned COMDEX this way before, and no company ever would again. Microsoft had reinvented and redefined the idea of "promotion," with tens of thousands of dollars in tips for hotel bell clerks and housekeeping staffs alone. (All those pillowcases didn't come cheap.) Microsoft had greased the palms of certain shift managers; other times it was a worker with a little entrepreneurial chutzpah.

"You'd be amazed by the power held by doormen, head maids, housekeepers, and security guards," Hanson said. "As well as the leads limo drivers can give you."

In total, Microsoft would spend $450,000. After that, COMDEX put policies in place requiring that companies go through the proper channels if they wanted paraphernalia in hotel rooms.

From that point on, Gates did all of the announcements related to Windows, which seemed fitting, inasmuch as, by PR edict, he would personally get all the credit.

At Gates's keynote speech, the lights dimmed, and a spotlight followed him to center stage in front of a standing-room-only audience. His fingerprint-smudged glasses reflected the light. Dandruff dusted his collar. He looked like central casting's idea of a technical genius, which was, of course, all part of the image being marketed.

So when Gates stood there and promised that Microsoft would ship Windows in the spring of 1984, people believed him. The company had just spent hundreds of thousands of dollars to launch it, so of course it would ship.

However, the developers actually doing the work back in Bellevue knew that the truth was something quite different. Eller, Wood, and Remala, especially, knew the product would never ship by April of 1984, because, of course, Windows was the true archetype of that soon to be prevalent term "vaporware." Gates's COMDEX demo was little more than a videotape that flashed graphics on the screen in different windows. It barely contained any code, and what little code it did contain was riddled with bugs, but it looked better than VisiOn's demo, and in this age of image, that's what counted.

In Microsoft's initial surveys of COMDEX attendees arriving at the Las Vegas airport, only 10 percent of those polled had even heard of Windows, and no one understood what it was or why it was important. When Hanson's team conducted their exit polls, public perception and awareness for Microsoft and Windows had grown to 90 percent—in one week.

The company received its first television coverage, and people held off on VisiOn, waiting instead for Windows 1.0—the safe, quality buy. Developers started calling VisiCorp, "VisiCorpse."

Microsoft crushed VisiOn and built infallible momentum for Windows. The Soft would emerge as a completely different company, not based on its technical merit, but on its marketing prowess.

Gates would emerge a different person as well. He was on his way to pop-icon status. But a casualty of this change would be the attention he could pay to his technical people and to the actual development of Windows. Ironically, never had the programmer-CEO been less involved in his company's programming.

This lack of involvement would wreck havoc during the entire two-year period it would take to get Windows out the door.

3

. . . .

BE LIKE THE MAC

Good thing I'm here. I'll have this looking like
the Mac in no time!

—*Neil Konzen*

In the early eighties, while Microsoft was first learning to flex its
marketing muscle, the darling of Wall Street was a little start-up
based in Cupertino, California.

Apple Computer, cofounded in 1976 by an arrogant and irreverent marketing genius named Steve Jobs, and a technical visionary
named Steve Wozniak, had set out to develop proprietary personal-
computer systems for businesses, schools, and the home. Its machines would be completely incompatible with the IBM PC. The
company went public in 1980, and two years later it became the
first PC maker to reach an annual sales rate of $1 billion.

In 1981, Jobs began a secret project—a new graphical computer,
dubbed the Macintosh, which Jobs would tout as the "computer for
the rest of us."

Apple was building all the new hardware for the Mac as well as
the Mac operating system, but Jobs approached Bill Gates about
building applications. Apple was tired of paying $75 for every copy
of VisiCalc, the spreadsheet it licensed from VisiCorp, and wanted a
cheaper solution.

Gates jumped at the opportunity, and he was bowled over when

Jobs showed him a prototype of the Mac, mesmerized by the computer's graphics, buttons, and menus that flashed on the screen. In Gatespeak, it was *really cool,* and dollar signs reflected in the lenses of those now famous Gates eyeglasses. He knew that building desktop applications for the Mac would be a huge revenue source for Microsoft, and the deal with Apple was inked.

According to the developers on the Windows team, Gates didn't view Apple or the Mac as a competitor to Microsoft, and he never would. In Gates's mind, Apple was a hardware company, and Microsoft was a software company. The two would be the Dynamic Duo.

But in reality, Microsoft was also a maker of operating systems, and hence, a potential competitor to Apple. To build desktop applications for the Macintosh, Microsoft developers needed access to its application programming interfaces. APIs were the unique way the application communicated with the Mac operating system. As part of the Jobs-Gates deal, the APIs were to be kept confidential until the Mac shipped.

At Microsoft's Bellevue campus, Apple's new machine was afforded the reverence of an extraterrestrial brought back to the lab. So other developers passing by couldn't see in, the developers working on the software for the Mac used paper to cover the office windows that faced out onto the corridor.

Inside, the Microsoft team sat at the Mac testing their code. It was something of a leap of faith that Apple had given this business to Microsoft in the first place. These would be the very first mainstream applications for the new computer, and Microsoft had a lot at stake. With their chins down, their bodies hunched over the keyboard, they typed until their hands ached. When the Mac was introduced in January of 1984, Microsoft's applications would ship with it.

Protecting the APIs and the Mac specs was serious business for both companies. If the developers building Windows looked at that code, Microsoft could be in violation of its agreement with Apple. Gates took this issue seriously, creating a so-called Chinese Wall or information block between those Microsoft developers working on the Macintosh applications and those working on the Windows operating system. The papered-over windows and locked doors meant "Don't ask."

But programmers will be programmers. Developers on the Windows team had friends building applications for the Mac. Windows developers like Eller knew that behind one of the locked doors was a machine from Apple, just as it was common knowledge among developers that IBM's new PC, code-named Salmon, was behind another one. And as Windows team manager Scott McGregor would later recall, Gates was always complaining, "Why isn't this like the Mac?" and "Be more like the Mac," long before the Mac even shipped. This was a mantra that would become numbingly familiar in the months ahead.

As per the agreement, as soon as the Mac hit the street in late January 1984, the "Chinese Wall" fell down, and the code of silence was lifted.

When the Mac hit the streets, the world also discovered why Gates had been captivated when he first saw Apple's new machine back in 1981—the graphical user interface.

Though there were mixed reviews, overall, the bottom line was the same: the Mac would forever change the face of the business. The *New York Times* called the Mac "a revolution in computing." The *Washington Post* echoed the sentiments: "Even if the Mac fails to sell in the millions and Apple simply becomes just another computer company, it's still a significant forerunner of what personal computers are destined to become."

The strange tension and paranoia that had lingered in Microsoft's halls suddenly dissipated. Until the Mac shipped, Gates had not provided any strategic direction to the Windows team. Until that point, he seemed to have no interest in it at all. But Gates no longer had to worry about his Mac applications developers leaking to his Windows developers. The Mac was fair game now. Hunting season was officially open.

The day the Mac shipped in January 1984, Gates told McGregor to run out and buy a Mac for the Windows developers.

"Reverse engineer it," Gates told him. "I have applications like BASIC and Multiplan that we've hacked out for the Mac, and we're working on other Mac applications like Word with a graphical user interface. I want to run all those Mac applications on Windows."

Apparently, Gates didn't see a conflict of interest with this strategy. According to Eller, it wasn't a conscious decision to squash Apple, it was a business decision so Microsoft wouldn't have to write its applications twice. Which did seem logical. Gates didn't want two sets of applications, one for the Mac and one for Windows. That would require twice the man power, twice the investment, and twice the time. Furthermore, Gates was enamored with the Mac, so why shouldn't his Windows team build a Mac-like system for the IBM PC?

But after carefully looking at the Macintosh, the Windows developers knew the likelihood of running Mac applications on Windows was near zip. While both Microsoft's and Apple's systems were graphical, the guts of the two were completely different.

McGregor told Gates as much.

"How are they different?" Gates snapped back. "They both draw fucking lines on the screen, right? They both put things in windows, right? Mac wrote a windows thing, you wrote a windows thing, they ought to be able to run the same stuff together."

Which is when it became clear to Eller that Gates still didn't have a clue as to how the Mac system worked.

Unlike the Mac, the Windows system was a new world order in which the operating system software, not the applications, controlled the desktop. The Mac was completely the opposite.

With the Mac's "pull" model, the application ruled the world. It treated the operating system as a servant. In the Windows "push" environment, an ideology McGregor had brought with him from Xerox, the operating system was the center of the universe, applications were merely slaves.

Fine, Gates said. Simple enough. Change the Windows model to be like the Mac.

But if the Windows team changed the model to pull, the ship date would slip another year. Gates simply didn't understand the architectural issues because he had not been in on the development process.

"In order to look like and be compatible with the Mac," McGregor told him, "we have to do a complete rewrite of Windows."

Gates's response was, "You have to be compatible with the Mac. How much will the date slip?"

"Maybe the fall or winter . . ."

"That's ridiculous," Gates said. "We've got to ship. We have to beat out VisiOn. We've already promised this to OEMs."

Not to mention a half million dollar marketing blitz at COMDEX promising it to the world.

Eller knew that Gates was dreaming. The Mac code and the Windows code were completely incompatible. The Mac was also completely incompatible with the IBM PC and with DOS, Microsoft's bread-and-butter source of revenues. Even if they went through all this Sturm und Drang, Windows would still not run Mac applications.

But Gates had the Mac bee in his war bonnet.

If McGregor and his Windows team couldn't make Windows run like the Mac, Gates would find someone who could.

Gates revered Neil Konzen as a Macintosh god. Konzen, a self-proclaimed Mac bigot, was one of the developers who had spent time behind the locked door at Microsoft helping to build their first applications for the Macintosh. Konzen was one of the few developers at Microsoft who had been on the other side of the Chinese Wall, with access to the Mac's application programming interfaces all along, and who, therefore, had intimate knowledge of the system.

Gates drafted Konzen to the Windows project.

"Good thing I'm here," Konzen told Eller. "I'll have this looking like the Mac in no time!"

Eller and his team had written what they felt was some very good Windows code. When Konzen came over he appeared to want to counter this impression—he told the Windows team their code was garbage. They had completely misengineered the system, he said.

"These Apple guys really know their graphics," Konzen told Eller. "They're better, faster, and simply easier to use. You chimps working on Windows don't have a clue."

One day Eller was in his office programming when the door swung open and Konzen and Gates appeared.

Eller looked up, thinking, This is exactly what I need.

Konzen had been in a few days earlier twisting Eller's arm to include some functions in Windows's graphical device interface, functions which Eller had assured him were not needed. Eller felt that if Konzen strongly believed these features were necessary, then Konzen could write them himself, but as far as he was concerned, they had nothing to do with GDI.

Konzen didn't bother going to McGregor. After all, McGregor was the one who had championed the un-Mac-like features in Windows that Konzen had been sent over to fix.

Instead, Konzen had marched straight to the chairman's office and grabbed the Bill himself. "I hear the graphics guy isn't building the right code and that you have an attitude problem," Gates told Eller. "I hear that you don't care how fast the graphics are or how easy they are for customers to use."

Eller blew up.

"I've been busting my ass twelve hours a day trying to get to the point that we have something we can ship and you're in here telling me that I don't care about the software?"

"Oh yeah?" Konzen said. "The region code is slow. On the Mac, the region code is super fast. You can do everything with regions. That's why their paint program is so fast."

"Bullshit," Eller countered. "Paint uses bitmaps. If they used regions you'd see speed differences based on screen complexity and you don't. They use bitmaps. Besides, I already told you, the region code currently works. It's written in C. We can speed it up later, after we're functionally complete."

"Yeah," Konzen said. "But it has to be really fast. Regions are what makes the Mac so great."

"Wrong. They tell you that and you believe it," Eller said. "Regions are not the beginning and the end of graphics, they're just one little component. I don't give a fuck about regions!"

"See, Bill?" Konzen said. "He doesn't care about making the code fast."

"Maybe I should get someone in here who really does care about the graphics code," Gates said.

"Yeah, why don't you do that," Eller told him.

Eller knew Gates wasn't going to find anyone to take over the graphics code. Eller also knew that the only way to deal with Gates was to stand up to him. Increasingly, the kind of people Gates chewed up for lunch or breakfast were "yes" people.

"Boy, do I ever hate this job," Eller thought. "God, just let me finish this miserable code."

Eller wasn't the only one on the team hating his job. Almost all the key developers on the project thought of quitting or even tried to resign at least once. But not many actually did. Back then, the attrition rate was very low because people believed in the Windows vision. They believed that the software they were writing would revolutionize the world.

This was the most brutal argument Gates and Eller would ever have, but by no means the last one. The next debate would not be about the Mac or Eller's code, but about a small, innovative software company in Mountain View, California.

• • •

Shortly after Eller began working on GDI, McGregor brought in his ex–Xerox PARC buddy John Warnock for a meeting at Microsoft. Warnock had set up a graphics and languages software company called Adobe Systems, Inc. McGregor wanted to discuss Adobe's new system that competed with GDI. Competition meant a possible threat to Microsoft, which meant Microsoft just might be interested in Warnock's technology.

Donned in jeans and a T-shirt, Eller sat in with the execs and reviewed Adobe's graphics technology called PostScript. He read through the documentation, and his jaw dropped.

Microsoft was toast. Eller had been programming GDI and was happy with his progress, but when he looked at Adobe's PostScript, he was in awe. It was truly beautiful. Compared to PostScript, GDI was a bag of crap.

PostScript had a unity of design that was breathtaking. Concepts and code were reused, graphics and text were integrated in a single model. In Apple's QuickDraw and in Microsoft's own GDI, when fonts scaled they became irregular, fat, and ugly, but in PostScript the fonts scaled up smoothly. With PostScript, the images that came off the printer mimicked what was on the computer screen. This was what Microsoft should have been building all along.

Still, Adobe didn't deal with color, and neither did the Mac. Windows did. Also, whereas Eller had been optimizing his GDI program so that images appeared on-screen quickly, Adobe didn't try to do anything fast. Adobe hadn't dealt with issues on the computer screen, like moving mouse cursors, but, then again, it did print. Neither Eller nor the rest of the Windows group had even looked at the issue of printing.

Eller gazed into Adobe's PostScript technology and saw Windows clouding over. He wanted to fuse these two models together and do some joint development, but how? That would set back the Windows schedule even further while they tried to hook Adobe's code into Windows's GDI graphics. Still, Eller believed Microsoft should work with Adobe. But Eller and McGregor also knew that if they wanted final approval to go ahead with Adobe, they needed to include Gates.

Unfortunately, Gates, still fixated on the Mac, had other ideas.

At the next meeting, Warnock sat down and explained to Gates how Adobe's technology worked and how the graphics looked. Gates peered through those smudged eyeglasses and kept asking, "Why would anybody want any of this? What the world wants is Apple's QuickDraw. They've already spoken—QuickDraw is excellent. QuickDraw does all this cool stuff. The graphics look great, and it's fast."

Apple had designed its software and its hardware concurrently. The dots on the Macintosh screen, the pixels, and those on the Apple printer were perfect squares exactly the same size. That was why screen images and print images looked identical on Apple's system. The only printer you could get for the Apple computer was an Apple printer.

In the computer world, however, it wasn't that simple. In the world of PCs there were hundreds of other printers made by various manufacturers. Each had its own printer driver, and every printer printed documents differently, and what people saw on their computer screens was not necessarily what came off the printer. Many software applications wouldn't print on certain printers.

Adobe's PostScript technology, on the other hand, provided a uniform way for all applications and all printers to talk. But Gates still didn't care. It might be uniform, it might look good, but it would be too slow. It didn't have the word *quick* in the name!

Warnock shook his head and left.

Eventually, PostScript would become the standard for printing documents, and Adobe would become one of the largest companies in the software industry.

Gates's refusal to adopt Adobe's technology had something to do with money—Gates was not feeling cash rich in 1984—but it had even more to do with Gates's persistent delusion that Windows be like the Mac.

For example, the group had originally designed their own scroll bar, but it wasn't like the Mac's. With the Windows scroll bar, people got an extra visual representation. The thumb on the right-hand side of the page changed size based on how much of the document they were seeing. With the Mac, the thumb size didn't change.

"That's not compatible with the Mac," Gates said. "It's got to be like the Mac."

Other features that had been designed into Windows under McGregor were also being questioned. No matter if they were better, if they weren't like the Mac, Gates wanted them taken out. So the scroll bar was changed to match the Mac's.

Early Windows prototypes featured drag and drop for copying and pasting, which was ordered removed because the Mac didn't do it.

These were not necessarily all bad decisions. They simply had the effect of further delaying a product that had already been whacked off into the weeds.

A particular sore point between the Windows team and the duo of Gates and Konzen was the debate between tiled and overlapped windows. McGregor, religious in his fervor for tiling, wasn't going to budge.

When windows overlapped, as they did on the Mac, one window ended up on top of the other. It looked like a stack of papers on the computer screen, and as a result, McGregor said, people spent all of their time dragging windows around to uncover what was hidden. With tiled windows, all the windows were visible at the same time. The windows always filled the screen, getting smaller as more windows were opened.

"We did the studies at PARC to decide which system required

less mouse motion to accomplish a fixed goal," McGregor said. "Tiled was always more efficient."

But efficient didn't necessarily mean sexy.

"The computer press at the time was beating us up for being lazy and not doing the work to do overlapped windows," Eller said. "What they didn't realize was that we already *had* overlapped windows. Dialogs and menus are overlapped windows. We had written a lot of code to do tiling so that the system would be more efficient for users. Unfortunately, tiling didn't look as cool as overlapped windows, and we found that looking cool was more important to consumers than efficiency."

Konzen, the Mac guy, was adamant about getting rid of tiled windows, but he knew he didn't have time to take them out. Instead, he added a feature that would allow people to view windows as overlapped.

Meanwhile, Konzen continued to tell the Windows team how to write code. At the same time, he was busily trying to hack up Windows so that it would run in the pull model like the Mac rather than in the push model the Windows team had originally developed.

Konzen was causing fights on a regular basis, and Eller began to doubt that the product would ever ship.

"There was a period when the bickering got so bad I sensed most of my team hated Neil," Eller said. "Neil was so depressed with what was going on that he decided he'd move to another project."

"These guys were already in death march before I show up," Konzen said. "Back then, a year or two years was a damn long time for a software project. Nobody was happy. Bill wasn't going down and saying, 'This is awesome.' What Bill was doing was going down and seeing us on the Mac, saying, 'Fuck, this is kickass.' Then he goes and sees their bag of shit . . . and so he never gave the team any satisfaction out of it."

McGregor was well aware of the friction. But McGregor also

knew that it was Gates who had ordered Windows on this Mac quest, and that Konzen was Bill's guy.

Finally the tension between the developers came to a head. McGregor had built a case against Konzen and wanted him moved off the Windows team.

Konzen himself said it was a very difficult time. McGregor repeated this to Ballmer, who in turn agreed to talk to Konzen.

Most of the Windows guys were elated. They said, "Cool, Neil's going to quit! This is great! He's finally going down there to talk to Ballmer, and we'll finally be rid of that son of a bitch, and we can get back to getting our system ready."

But the meeting took hours. Why was it taking so long?

Then Ballmer came back in. "I've got good news!" he announced in his booming voice.

The developers smiled.

"I just sat down and had a long chat with Neil," Ballmer explained. "We've talked about the problems that have arisen between him and the rest of the group, and we have resolved them. I've convinced Neil to stay on the team. I talked him into it, and he's not going to leave. You get to keep your star slugger right here at the plate."

Konzen stayed on the Windows project and continued his path of destruction. Day by day, the ship dates for Windows slipped further and further behind. April came and went. Now Microsoft was promising that Windows would ship in November of 1984. But all along the developers knew it was never going to happen.

In the summer of 1984, Steve Wood went to McGregor's office to apprise him of the situation.

"We aren't going to make it," Wood said. "There's no way we're going to ship in time for COMDEX. It just isn't going to happen. We're so far away it's pathetic."

As Wood later recalled, McGregor simply didn't want to hear the bad news. McGregor just wanted to keep marching along on the big mac-denial death march, assuming all would work out for the best.

And then Gates received the *really* bad news: Windows categorically was *not* going to be like the Mac.

He was apoplectic. The company had already missed their highly advertised spring 1984 launch; now the fall ship date might not happen either. And all Microsoft had to show for their delays was a product the developers themselves acknowledged was simply a poor man's version of the Mac.

Gates's preoccupation with the Mac cost the Windows team seven to eight months of valuable development time. The developers, while trying to appease Gates, were precluded from building a product that had its own identity. But even when Gates realized Windows wasn't going to be what he wanted, instead of giving the team a chance to retrench and get on with it, he loosened up his pitching arm to throw one more monkey wrench into the works.

4

· ·

DEATH MARCH

Thanks for the tip, bud, we'll keep it in mind.
                                    —*Marlin Eller*

By August 1984, the Windows team was on the verge of despair. Programmers talked among themselves, trying to figure out some way to cut their losses and just ship. Customers who chose to forgo VisiOn in anticipation of Windows were getting pissed and voicing their complaints in the press. Those people who had seen what they thought were demos of an actual product were even more put off.

But while the computer press fumed, most of the other hardware and software manufacturers rationalized the delays. Publicly they maintained that it was better for Microsoft to fix any problems first, even if it meant waiting to ship. Some even praised Microsoft for its restraint. It was public relations positioning at its finest.

Then, three months before Windows was scheduled to go out the door, Gates decided he could no longer ignore one key point hardware makers had been hammering into him for months. They didn't want the Windows system to be solely reliant on the mouse.

Customers just didn't like mice, the manufacturers said. It was a foreign concept. Most people didn't understand what to do with a mouse. Sure, it was a great option, but executives were used to keyboards—not mice. They wanted familiar commands like Alt Tab or Shift F1 to move the cursor around the screen.

Gates ordered that the mouse be exterminated, which, of course, completely contradicted his earlier diktat to make Windows exactly like the Mac. The fact was, if you used a Mac, you had to use a mouse. And that was exactly the way the team designed Windows. Now all that had to be changed.

While time consuming, mouse control was not a difficult fix. But then Gates really decided to stir up a shit storm.

Up until this point, IBM had always been Microsoft's largest ally in the PC industry. It licensed and installed more copies of Microsoft's DOS operating system than any other hardware vendor. And this was *IBM*, the predominant PC maker in the industry, a key alliance for anyone. Gates had done much lobbying to get IBM to support Windows, but Big Blue wasn't budging. As it turned out, IBM was developing a potential competitor—a twenty-pound Butterball named TopView.

Since introducing the PC in 1981, IBM had relied solely on Microsoft's DOS operating system. Since then, other companies had been cloning the PC and licensing DOS from Microsoft. Now, perhaps, it was time for IBM to wean itself from Microsoft and regain control of the PC operating-system market.

In August 1984, IBM announced their new character-based multitasking shell—TopView—which they positioned as the upgrade to DOS. But it was also the *alternative* to Windows. IBM, which had no plans to license TopView to other vendors, was making a run at creating the new, de facto standard in the marketplace.

TopView was the epitome of IBM—clunky, anticonsumer, and abysmally slow. It ate up precious computer memory. Moreover, because it didn't sport a graphical user interface, it would have no appeal to the vastly untapped mainstream consumer market. But TopView did allow for multitasking, running multiple applications at one time and switching back and forth among them, a feature high on IBM's priority list.

Because of TopView's lack of a graphical user interface, the

Microsoft team shrugged it off as a nonthreat—everyone, that is, except Gates. TopView's very existence shook him to the core. Gates knew better than anyone else just how much IBM's reflected glory meant to Microsoft. By endorsing DOS in 1981, IBM had instantaneously turned Microsoft into a major player. So overwhelming was IBM's strength in the marketplace that it could probably market TopView, with all its flaws, and still squash Windows and any other competitor before lunch.

If Microsoft wanted to continue riding Big Blue's coattails, Gates had better *support* TopView pronto, i.e., build Windows so that it could be run on this new IBM platform. But supporting TopView meant including support for DOS applications, vestiges of the old IBM platform. Microsoft had claimed Windows would do this.

In reality, it didn't.

"Your DOS compatibility sucks!" Gates told the developers.

The developers still had not received a clear directive on whether Windows would subsume DOS, be an application that ran on top of DOS, or be just a little graphics subroutine library. Supreme Techlord William Gates should have provided this strategic direction early on, but he did not.

"There was no strategic direction from Bill and Ballmer about these two things," recalled Steve Wood. "It was like, 'Well we have these two things, DOS and Windows, and do we have to run on top of this new multitasking DOS? Are we running on top of DOS 3.0 and we just ignore those guys?' That went on for a year, this lack of strategic direction. And we just made our own decisions."

Gates had never been involved in any of the architectural design of Windows, nor had he ever been personally involved in writing such large amounts of code. Now, very late in the game, he was throwing out knee-jerk requests based on the competition. And he seemed totally oblivious to the fact that every such feature change radically screwed up Windows's stability, testing, and ship date.

The Windows programmers began hacking away on TopView

compatibility, but down in the team's collective gut, they knew there wasn't a snowball's chance in San Diego that they were going to ship Windows by fall of 1984.

Morale was heading south. Developers were burning out. Family relationships suffered greatly.

In June of 1984, Steve Wood's younger brother, who was also his best friend, suddenly died. This key Windows developer was understandably devastated. Wood went to Gates's second-in-command, Ballmer, and told him he wanted to quit.

At least the VP appreciated talent and continuity in the face of deadlines. "Okay, we'll make you a consultant," Ballmer told Wood.

"What do you make as a consultant?"

"We'll double your salary," Ballmer said.

Wood's salary immediately jumped from $35,000 to $70,000 a year.

"We'll make you a consultant, and we'll leave all your benefits alone. We'll just pretend that you're a consultant," Ballmer said. "And when we're done with Windows you come back, and we'll see about how we can get you to stay here."

Confused, Wood told Ballmer he'd think about the offer. Wood didn't like the idea of leaving something unfinished, so he convinced himself to stay.

In August, Ballmer, the former Harvard sports guy, boomed out one of his "rah-rah" pep speeches to the Windows team, talking about how Windows would ship in 1984 at the fall COMDEX.

The developers tried to conceal their laughter. No one had bothered to tell Ballmer that the schedule was nuts.

Shortly thereafter, Gates decided to restructure not only the group, but the entire company.

Microsoft set up a systems software division, which Ballmer would head, and a business applications division, which would focus on desktop applications such as word processors. The official Microsoft pronouncement said that this reorganization would enable Gates to focus on product development instead of day-to-day operations. In truth, Gates needed to be more outwardly focused—sales and marketing, corporate relations—and Ballmer needed to concentrate on getting Windows out the door. The two were determined to get the project back in line and on track toward some reasonable timetable.

"Gates and Ballmer started saying that Scott didn't understand the PC industry," Eller recalled. "He'd been making the wrong design decisions, clearly, which is why Bill had to step in and fix things. Furthermore, Bill thought Scott simply had been lying about the time schedules. Scott had said Windows would ship in April, and it didn't. Then he promised September, and we didn't ship in September. But Bill simply wasn't factoring in the impact of his demands on the system."

So McGregor would no longer report directly to Gates, but would be answering to Ballmer.

Ballmer and McGregor's management styles clashed from day one. Ballmer's modus operandi for dealing with technical issues was to pound on the developers until they caved in to his own unrealistic expectations of what the ship date should be.

This, on top of the fact that engineers are overly optimistic by nature, was a prescription for disaster. McGregor knew that when Wood or Eller promised that a feature would be finished in two months, it would be complete in four. In Ballmer's naively managerial mind-set, if Wood said it would take two months, then in reality it could be done in one—if only people would get fired up.

In one case, Steve Wood wanted to redo the memory management system because it was slow and riddled with bugs. Ballmer agreed it should be rewritten, but McGregor warned him, "I guarantee it's a minimum three month slip if you touch the memory manager. It takes that amount of time just to make it stable again."

Ballmer wasn't convinced. He and Gates immediately began the none-too-subtle process of shoving McGregor aside.

In September, with Ballmer in control, the death march began. Developers worked seven days a week, setting dates and never making them, but never really missing them by terribly much.

Toward the end of the project, Eller spent almost no time writing code, and instead spent all of his time fending off outsiders who were trying to come in and add to his work list.

Gates had planned to have Microsoft applications such as Excel ready to ship when Windows went out the door. So the applications group began telling the Windows team they needed new code added to Windows so their applications would work. Eller's usual response to requests was, "Thanks for the tip, bud, we'll keep it in mind for the next version."

This earned him the nickname "Dr. No."

Eller considered one of his responsibilities, as a development lead, to be controlling the temperature of the development process. The early days of a project were considered to be "hot." As a proper development lead, Eller listened to ridiculous propositions. And if the other team members belittled an idea by saying, "That's the stupidest idea I've ever heard," Eller encouraged them not to be hasty. Perhaps there was some more clever way of doing whatever needed to be done. Eller turned off his internal editor and entertained any idea. But then as time went on and things weren't moving along and people continued to argue, he'd rein in the options and push for unanimity.

But how could they ever reach consensus when the entire direction of Windows 1.0 was unclear from the get go and when radical changes were continually being thrown at them by Chairman Bill himself?

It was also true that technology simply continued to evolve—rapidly. In 1984, few people owned hard drives. Since Windows had been intended for shipment that year, it was targeted to a 256KB PC with two floppy disks and no hard drive required. But as the group got closer to the ultimate ship date, which still wouldn't be for at least another twelve months, Windows had bloated in size and now required a PC with a hard drive.

Coach Ballmer summoned his players into the huddle.

"Obviously we aren't making fall COMDEX," he said. "We need to find out where we're at, where we have to be, and then come up with some real dates that we can meet."

The developers responded with a collective "No shit, Sherlock."

Then Ballmer went off to do damage control about COMDEX.

Fortunately, Microsoft hadn't planned for a repeat of their 1983 launch extravaganza. The developers had known all along that they didn't have a prayer of shipping Windows by the fall, but Microsoft wouldn't tell the public this until late October, and it has never to this day let the press know the real reasons why.

The job of doling out the apologies fell to Microsoft's group manager of systems products marketing, Leo Nikora.

"The speed, size, and performance is still not up to the standards that we've set for ourselves and that our customers have come to expect," Nikora told the press. "In light of all the work and support dedicated to Windows, we felt it was in everyone's best interest to not hurry things and do a better product."

Ballmer's designs on McGregor did not include firing him, because Gates worried that if McGregor left the project midstream, the press would find out and flame Microsoft in the papers. Gates begged him to stay for the "good of the project," just as long as he wasn't *in charge of* the project. Gates told McGregor he'd pay his full salary, and McGregor could do whatever he wanted. Gates would call McGregor an architect, which was the hip word at Microsoft, so long as he stayed at the company until Windows shipped.

McGregor left anyway. His attitude was, essentially, "Screw that. I'm not going to stay around and do nothing while you guys use me and mess up my project."

McGregor was told he could pick up his things in the parking garage the next day, and Ballmer physically moved into his office. Sadly, one of the things McGregor would leave behind was eight figures in Microsoft stock options.

With McGregor out of the picture, the Windows team was hurting for technical leadership as they struggled to solve all the remaining problems of DOS compatibility.

In addition to being a technical boomer in the woods, Ballmer was rarely around. A businessman, not a developer, he was always off talking to companies like IBM, and yet he insisted on being involved in every decision.

"Nobody makes any decisions without checking with me first," Ballmer told the group. "If you're going to change any of the interfaces or anything for that matter, you have to talk to me in order to get them approved. We'll improve communications this way."

On a good week, Ballmer might be in his office one day, maybe two. The rest of the time he was on the road selling.

Still, for Eller and Wood, getting approval was relatively easy. They would simply "explain" the feature they wanted to include. Ballmer obviously wouldn't understand the technical aspects, but he wouldn't let on. Instead, he would ask a few questions to show he was listening. The developers would continue telling Ballmer more than he wanted to know and laying out what it was they actually wanted to do, and Ballmer eventually would say yes.

To a few people, Ballmer said no just to prove he was top dog. But that was not the only way he would strive to mark his territory.

On Easter Sunday, 1985, Ballmer called a meeting.

"The energy was up, everyone was committed, it was great," Ballmer fondly recalled. He seemed to regard it as one of the highlights of his career. Eller and the others would remember it a little differently.

"Be there, nine A.M.," Ballmer ordered. And he didn't mean just the managers; he summoned the whole group.

"But that's *Easter Sunday*." Eller said. "Some folks might want to go to church."

"Too bad," Ballmer said. "We have to have a status meeting."

Ballmer made it painfully clear that the only purpose of the status meeting was to see who was committed to the project and who wasn't. He also let it be known that he'd be taking down the names of those who showed up for this strange little ecumenical service and those who didn't.

On Easter morning, roughly twenty-five people dragged their butts into the conference room. They weren't happy as they sat down with Ballmer to go over the feature list.

"So how's the status of Windows?" Ballmer asked.

"Not much different than it was last night, Steve," Eller assured him. "We're still working on the same things we were working on at midnight last night."

"Okay," Ballmer said. "Good, then. Press on."

Not even Catbert, Evil HR Director, could have topped this one.

To Ballmer, the meeting was a symbolic gesture, a test of commitment. And Ballmer loved the excitement of dealing with a crisis. Having a meeting on Easter Sunday—now *that* was crisis management.

Despite these Dilbertesque failings, Ballmer may have been just the guy to champion this project. Like every great salesman, Ballmer could charge into meetings and immediately raise the crowd's temperature with his booming voice. He'd become animated, waving his hands in the air and telling everyone how important their work was to the world. He infused a contagious energy, and many developers thrived on this "mission from God" intensity. They truly believed they were doing something that would revolutionize the world.

Ultimately, Ballmer said that Windows would ship before the last leaf fell off the autumn trees, and in time for COMDEX. In November 1985, Windows at long last made it out the door.

In honor of the event, Pam Edstrom, who had since left Microsoft to cofound her own agency, Waggener Edstrom, and handle Microsoft's PR from the outside, sponsored a "Windows Roast." Gathered at the Alexis Park Resort in Las Vegas, Gates and Ballmer made fun of themselves and not so subtly apologized for the Windows delays. "To Dream the Impossible Dream" was the theme song playing in the background. With three hundred analysts and members of the press invited to these festivities where Gates and Ballmer let it all hang out, it was another coup for "Gates's Keeper."

Gates joked that Ballmer had insisted, " 'We just gotta cut features.' He came up with this idea that we could rename this thing Microsoft Window—and we would have shipped that thing a long time ago."

Stewart Alsop, industry gadfly, presented Gates with the "Golden Vaporware" award, saying, "The delay of Windows was all part of a secret plan to have Bill turn thirty before it shipped."

By the time Windows 1.0 rolled out, the software took up a whopping 512K of memory. But as the *New York Times* reviewer wryly observed, "Running Windows in 512K of memory is akin to pouring molasses in the Arctic."

So much for Microsoft's promise not to ship until Windows's bloated size had been gotten under control.

But to the public at large, Gates and company kept a poker face, adhering to their newly spun credo of image marketing, even though the applications for the new system were nowhere to be seen. Not even Microsoft itself had brought any new applications to the party. Windows was suffering from the classic chicken and egg syndrome—people weren't going to write applications until there was an installed base of PCs on the market running the new operating system.

Of those who, ostensibly, had waited years to purchase Windows 1.0, few actually pulled out the credit card. Those who did were less than impressed. Windows was being called nothing more than a "patch" to DOS, and a poor patch at that. Multitasking, one of Windows's much touted features, wasn't even useful to most consumers. And yet, the press asked, if people weren't using multitasking, why would anyone buy the product?

"Windows is also an extremely memory-hungry piece of software," reviewer Erik Sandberg-Diment of the New York Times News Service wrote. "According to the package copy, it requires a minimum of 256K of RAM. Even the 512K of RAM recommended in the Windows manual is not sufficient for the program to run with any alacrity."

The Windows package also claimed that users could use either a keyboard or a mouse to initiate commands, but as Sandberg-Diment added, "It seems to me that you really need a mouse for this program. There are keyboard commands, but to execute one of them you must first press the Alt key to display the command menu, then press the down arrow key until you reach the command you want on the display and highlight it, and then press Enter."

Like Disneyland, Windows had been designed with a mouse in mind.

The mere fact that Windows 1.0 came to market was a phenomenon in and of itself. For the three years leading up to the final shipment, life had been hell for the Microsoft programmers. As they ruefully acknowledged to one another, they had brought to market a project that had no identity of its own. Instead, it was like "Sybil," a case of multiple personalities, none of which got along with the others particularly well. Windows didn't support either Mac or TopView applications, and DOS compatibility was a joke.

In short, the product was essentially useless.

Gates would leave in place a tiny three-man team to nurse Windows along, but the maimed and much maligned project would slip to last place on his priority list. IBM was far more the burr under Gates's blanket. Big Blue still showed no signs of supporting Windows, and without IBM's seal of approval, Windows's future looked grim.

This was hardly an auspicious beginning for what would become one of the most successful products of all time.

5

· ·

ANYTHING FOR IBM

Get the business, get the business, get the business.
—*Steve Ballmer*

After three years of crippling stress in Bellevue, Gates wasn't the only person with a new agenda. Most of the Windows team took a month off. Many wanted to quit. Some actually did. Eller decided to take a working sabbatical in Japan.

While Eller had been finishing up Windows, his wife, Mary, had been finishing her Ph.D. in statistics. Unfortunately, she completed her doctorate the same year Reagan shut down the Department of Housing and Urban Development, the primary employer of such social scientists. Suddenly, academic departments were talking about layoffs instead of hiring. Depressed, Mary began searching for other opportunities, and eventually, she found a job doing statistics in Hiroshima, Japan.

Formal procedures for taking sabbaticals would not be developed for another eleven years at Microsoft, but special situations could be negotiated with Gates and Ballmer. Eller managed to convince them to let him work for Microsoft in Japan.

Before going overseas, Eller met with his bosses to discuss which projects he would work on and what E-mail hooks he could get into Microsoft. Eller's usual sessions with Gates had been project up-dates. They were either group meetings, or it was Gates alone in

Eller's office, chewing him out because Konzen had sent in the boss to get a yes from Dr. No.

But now Eller and Ballmer met with Gates in the chairman's office. Gates seemed pretty straightforward. It was Ballmer who seemed to be a totally different person. Gone was Mr. Bombast, and in his place was an obsequious yes-man. Anything Gates said, Ballmer toadied up to.

The usual booming Ballmer voice dropped ninety-nine decibels to normal conversational tones. The flamboyant salesman calmly asked questions, such as, "What do you think of that, Bill?"

Clearly Gates ran the show, not Ballmer. If Gates said, "I think we should look into that," Ballmer took it as an order. "Fine sir, that's an action item for me, I'll be doing that right away."

Ultimately, Gates and Ballmer agreed to let Eller live in Japan for two years and to continue working on Windows code.

Meanwhile, Eller's Windows partner, Steve Wood, was also once again pondering his future at Microsoft. He had dutifully fulfilled his promise to Ballmer and held on until Windows shipped. But the question was now, as Wood asked Ballmer, "Why should I stay?"

"I want you to stay because I want you to go sell IBM on Windows," Ballmer told him. "I want you to help get the IBM deal."

"We all know what it's like to work with IBM," Wood said. "It's going to be a no-fun job. And if I'm going to be stuck in a no-fun job for a couple years, I want to be a millionaire when it's over."

Wood, thinking his Microsoft stock might be worth $10 a share one day, told Ballmer he'd stay if they would come up with 100,000 options for him. Ballmer didn't deliver quite that much, but given splits and growth of 24,500 percent, let's just say he made it well worth his while.

From the beginning, though, sparks flew between the Microsoft programmer and the blue-suited bureaucrats at IBM.

Programmers at Microsoft were used to showing up to work when they wanted, wearing what they wanted, and basically *doing* what they wanted. They didn't follow a nine-to-five schedule, they didn't wear suits, and they didn't take to authority, unless it was from Gates.

Not so at IBM. The standard protocol there since time immemorial—even for programmers—was starched white shirts, blue pants, and an equally stringent chain of development procedures.

If IBM executives wanted a product from Microsoft, Gates would promise it in a month or two, then leave it up to the developers to deliver.

This was fine with Wood and others . . . until IBM executives started asking questions the Softies couldn't answer.

"What is the policy for testing new products?"

Testing? This was the early 1980s. Microsoft didn't have formal testing procedures. When a developer got a version that compiled, they shipped it.

"Our policy is simple," Microsoft developers explained. "If a problem surfaces and a customer reports it, we'll fix it."

IBM executives were appalled. They demanded to talk to the program managers.

Microsoft didn't have any program managers.

If Microsoft didn't *have* program managers, the IBM executives wondered, how did the company write specifications for its products?

It didn't. The developers simply made sure their code worked. Then they put it on a disk and shipped it to IBM.

No regression tests to make sure that any changes in the code didn't break some other part of the software?

Nope.

IBM executives were dumbstruck.

If the products Microsoft delivered to IBM were so abominable, then why didn't IBM just build them themselves? Internally, the Microsoft developers knew the reason IBM delegated its work— IBM's highly regarded policies and procedures made them as slow as Christmas. It would take IBM a year to complete code that Microsoft could finish, the recent Windows experience notwithstanding, in a fraction of the time.

What IBM was actually buying, through its relationship with Microsoft, was a way out of its own rigid hierarchy and painfully slow development process. So IBM continued to deal with Microsoft and buy its tools and languages, including DOS, but they also continued to whine.

Conversely, Microsoft had a long tradition of swallowing their pride as they took IBM's money. Developers at Microsoft referred to this process as BOGU—"Bend Over and Grease Up." Then they added an *S* to BOGU to create BOGUS for "Bend Over and Grease Up, Steve," inasmuch as it was Ballmer who sealed most of the IBM deals.

Ballmer, in keeping with his verbal repetition fetish, was determined to "Get the business, get the business, get the business." He desperately wanted IBM to license Windows, but that was an endorsement IBM continued to withhold.

While IBM wasn't taking Windows, it was still taking DOS. In August 1985, as the Windows team put the finishing touches on their work, Gates signed another deal with IBM, renewing their longstanding vows. Gates said it was the biggest contract Microsoft had ever signed. The deal would help pave the way for Microsoft to raise $61 million in an initial public offering seven months later, in March 1986.

The two companies also agreed to jointly develop a next generation operating system, which would be called OS/2. The agreement alleviated the worries of some industry pundits that IBM was moving away from DOS and toward its own proprietary operating system.

DOS was about to enter its fifth version, and IBM and Microsoft were in deep discussions about its features and future. IBM desperately wanted a version of DOS that ran in "protected mode," which would give it the ability to execute multiple programs at once in a preemptive, multitasking fashion. This represented a radical break from the past.

DOS had been designed from the ground up as a nonprotected operating system that could only run in what was called "real mode," which is sort of like a zoo that can display only one animal at a time because it only has one cage. To keep one program from seeping into another and causing havoc, real mode restricted DOS to executing only one application in memory at a time—you have to close your database before opening your word processor. The "single cage" that created this limitation was the target microprocessor, the Intel 8088. The 8088, the central brain behind IBM's first-generation PCs, could only access about one megabyte of memory, hardly enough to run today's screen savers.

The problem with running in protect mode is that when one program starts seeping instructions into another, the computer crashes. Most PC users at the time didn't know or care about real mode or protect mode or preemptive multitasking features, but to IBM and its customers these capabilities were deemed critical. IBM's customers were big, blue-chip companies—real zoos—that relied on IBM's massive computer systems to run their businesses twenty-four hours a day, seven days a week. In these mission-critical environments, system failures or crashes, which were commonplace for PC users, were simply unacceptable. IBM wanted its customers to have IBM PCs that were as stable, robust, and secure as its larger systems. But with the current version of Microsoft's DOS, that was nothing more than a pipe dream.

Intel, for its part, helped move PC technology much closer toward IBM's vision when it introduced its next-generation 80286 microprocessor, which could access enough memory to display many different animals in many different cages at the same time. The 80286 could provide hardware support for multitasking, data security, and virtual memory—capabilities that were commonplace on larger computer systems at the time.

The weak link in all this advancing PC technology was DOS. In order for DOS to take advantage of Intel's new protect-mode chips, the operating system would have to be completely rewritten. But that would mean that all of the existing software programs that ran on top of DOS would be incompatible.

For Microsoft, pursuing a strategy that meant telling its customers that prior investments in DOS software would now be worthless was not a smart career move.

While Gates wasn't as enamored of preemptive multitasking as IBM, he was convinced the world would have to move to a protected-mode operating system. But he didn't want to go it alone, which led to the joint venture with IBM to develop the next generation of DOS, dubbed OS/2—a protected, preemptive multitasking version. Abandoning Microsoft's installed base of DOS users was a tough sell. Under such circumstances Big Blue was the perfect big brother to have on your side. People might not listen to Microsoft, but everyone would listen to IBM.

Amid all this uncertainty, IBM was still pushing TopView, something for which Microsoft had hoped—but failed—to include support in Windows.

Word trickled up of a company called Dynamical Systems Research (DSR) in Oakland, California, which was working on a product called Mondrian, which was exactly what Gates needed—a TopView clone.

The small company, with a group of Princeton physicists at the core, was working out of an attic rented from a guy named Darryl S. Rush, hence the name DSR. The group of developers had been conducting research, hacking away at a little windowing system to use for themselves. Perhaps someday they could sell it, but mostly it was just for laughs.

When IBM announced TopView, DSR found themselves chuckling indeed. They were sitting on a clone that had twice the speed and half the size. DSR knew that IBM wasn't going to license TopView to anyone else; they would keep it for themselves. This was DSR's opportunity to laugh all the way to the bank.

In the spring of 1986, Ballmer asked Wood to fly down and check out these clowns. Wood met the leader of the DSR clan, Nathan Myhrvold, and his brother Cameron, along with Dave Weise, Chuck Whitmer, Dave Anderson, and Wes Ruple.

After a full day at DSR, Wood was convinced. If Microsoft acquired the small company, it would not only be getting a smart bunch of guys, but the acquisition would allow Microsoft to check off the little box for IBM that said, "TopView support included."

Little did Wood know at the time, but DSR would arguably be Microsoft's single most important acquisition, changing the future of the company forever.

Wood flew back and met with Ballmer, who took the bait.

"These guys are good," Wood told Ballmer. "We should get them whatever it takes."

In June 1986, Microsoft bought DSR in a stock swap valued at an estimated $1.5 million.

When the developers from DSR arrived at Microsoft's new headquarters in Redmond, it was still unclear what they would work on. By this time, IBM had decided that maybe it didn't need TopView after all. It was a dog in the marketplace—the market wanted graphical interfaces.

It was also clear that IBM wasn't going to support Microsoft's Windows no matter what. IBM viewed Windows as a toy operating system. It only wanted OS/2.

But the world was moving to graphics, something that neither TopView nor OS/2 had. Why, then, wouldn't IBM sign up for Windows?

The answer lay in Hursley, England, where a group of IBMers were busily working on graphics for the next generation of OS/2, a system dubbed "Presentation Manager." It was going to be the protected-mode, preemptive multitasking version of DOS, with a graphics shell on top. It was also a bold attempt by IBM to regain control of the entire software industry, world without end, Amen.

IBM had licensed their mothership PC operating system, DOS,

from Microsoft, and consequently they did not derive as much revenue from it as they might have otherwise. And IBM had grown tired of sharing DOS with other computer manufacturers—nearly every PC vendor on the planet licensed the platform. If IBM and Microsoft jointly developed a graphical version of OS/2, IBM knew that Microsoft would sell the graphics software to IBM's competitors such as Compaq, just as Microsoft had done with DOS and Windows. But in 1986, the only OS/2 arrangement Microsoft had with IBM was to jointly develop the kernel, not the graphics.

In late summer, Gates and Ballmer at long last discovered this play for independence on IBM's part, and the duo leapt into intense negotiations with the managers at Hursley.

Not only was IBM insisting on doing their own graphics, now they were intent on changing the names of all the graphics APIs, making them totally incompatible with Windows. IBM used an API called GDDM (Graphical Data Display Manager), "God Damn" to those in the know, to connect to mainframes. They wanted something that would run across every platform, from mainframes to PCs and dumb terminals.

Microsoft developers thought this was absurd. Running the same graphics interface over mainframes, PCs, dumb terminals, and any other random platform IBM wanted to target was like having the same engine run the furnace and your wrist watch. But Microsoft kept these views to itself, still sucking up to IBM to get their business.

Wood hated the idea of making this gratuitous change to every API. On the other hand, as he later put it, "No one was using Windows anyway. It wasn't like there were a lot of people who were going to get hurt by this."

From August through November 1986, negotiations continued among IBM's group in Boca Raton, Florida, which owned the PC OS/2 operating system; IBM Hursley, which was going to own the graphical component; and Microsoft, which was essentially going to be the glue.

Whatever IBM wanted, Microsoft would do, even if it meant sacrificing its own products—including, perhaps especially, Windows.

After conceding to IBM by coming up with a draft spec and documenting all of the APIs IBM wanted, in December 1986, Microsoft finally got what *it* wanted. IBM and Microsoft would now jointly develop OS/2 Presentation Manager, a windowlike interface for OS/2.

It was a triumphant moment for Gates and company. They convinced the world that they had persuaded IBM to include a slightly modified version of Microsoft's own Windows program. Microsoft's marketing and public relations department was still positioning Windows as the platform that would dominate the desktop, especially as the industry moved to bigger, more powerful processors, namely Intel's 386 chip. IBM would use this chip to run OS/2 on its new line of computers.

In 1987, Scott Oki, Microsoft's director of marketing, told the press, "By establishing a single graphical user interface [Windows], we'll help everyone through the transition phase the industry is going through."

But in reality, IBM was still not supporting Windows, it was merely admitting it needed a graphical interface. IBM hadn't signed up for Windows, and OS/2 would not support Windows applications, but no one mentioned this.

With the IBM deal sewn up for both the graphics and the OS/2 kernel, why was Microsoft still doing Windows? After all, Ballmer and Gates said OS/2 would take over the majority of the machines by 1990.

Interviewed in 1995, Dave Weise, eight-year veteran Windows developer, explained the situation this way:

"We had no respect for installed base at this time. Since DOS had taken over so well, so quickly, any new operating system that was better was going to take over even faster. So at this point," Weise said, "Steve B [Ballmer] tried to kill Windows."

By December 1986, Wood had left the Windows project, as had most everyone else in the company. It was an orphaned piece of code that was destined for further abuse while Gates bet the company on OS/2.

Microsoft's applications group, however, saw OS/2 as hopelessly far off. They weren't developing applications for it—they still hadn't completed any applications for Windows, their previously overhyped operating-system strategy.

The term "operating-system strategy du jour" came into frequent use among all applications developers at this time. But Microsoft developers weren't the only ones shunning OS/2. Third-party software developers avoided it like the plague.

"How do I get Presentation Manager so I can start writing software applications when OS/2 PM isn't available yet?" they would ask.

Microsoft told them, "Write for Windows, write for Windows, write for Windows. Then when we have some OS/2 PM code you can use, you can port your application over to OS/2, and it will be simple."

We hope.

Just as Gates had convinced himself that Windows would be compatible with the Mac, he now believed OS/2 would be compatible with Windows, and this was the story Microsoft was telling.

The developers, like Wood, quickly realized that working on OS/2 would be another two-year death march. Jointly developing the first version of OS/2 with IBM had been difficult when there were just two groups, IBM Boca and Microsoft. But for OS/2 PM there would be four personalities to deal with—the Microsoft OS/2 team, headed by Wood's archrival, Gordon Letwin; Microsoft's OS/2 Program Manager group; IBM Boca; and IBM

Hursley. To make matters worse, none of these groups particularly liked each other.

The entire OS/2 Presentation Manager effort would be created by the committee from hell.

In May 1987, Peter Neupert, who would ultimately head up Microsoft's OS/2 graphics effort, called Steve Wood into his office.

"You got to go to Hursley," Neupert said. "We leave in two days."

"Well, that's fine," Wood told him. "But I'll need a divorce attorney when I get home. Our wedding anniversary is on May fifteenth, and my wife's taking me away on a secret vacation for the weekend."

"Ahh, no problem," Neupert explained. "Bring Gayle along, I'm doing the same with my wife."

Wood and his wife spent the weekend in London before the programmer had to go off to Hursley.

Wood and approximately eight people on Microsoft's OS/2 team spent three weeks in England, staying at a four-hundred-year-old hotel in Sparsholt called Laingston House.

Hursley itself was a mansion with a pedigree reaching back several centuries. The Spitfire fighter plane was designed there prior to the Second World War. The British had a crash design team, and they holed up there for months in the huge stone house surrounded by rolling fields and perfectly manicured grounds.

From the day the Microsoft crew arrived, their style clashed with the IBMers'. Disdainful of IBM's clunky hardware, the Microsoft team brought their own machines. Before long, true to their West Coast roots, the Americans were playing Frisbee out on the lawn, which brought the IBM security guard racing outside.

"You can't do that," the security guard told Wood.

"Why not?"

"The executive offices are right up there." The guard pointed to a sinister-seeming upstairs window. "They don't like seeing this kind of activity on their grass."

The security guards were further exercised when Wood and his team ordered pizza from a place in the nearby town of Winchester.

When the delivery man showed up at the Hursley mansion, the guards called Wood's team and they went down and tipped the delivery guy ten pounds. The driver was so grateful that Wood concluded he had never been tipped before. Wood and his comrades walked back through the corridors, carrying their pizzas, wearing their T-shirts and jeans, while all of the IBMers in blue suits and white shirts stared in disbelief.

But pizza and Frisbee were only fleeting diversions from the grim business at hand, three weeks of crisis management at the Hursley hellhole.

The IBMers couldn't get their part of the system to work, and the Microsoft developers thought Big Blue was clueless. Strangely, the IBMers lacked debugging skills. So Wood and his team spent three weeks hand-holding, helping the IBMers figure out how to get their software to work.

The Microsoft group made another trip to Hursley in July. Then the real crunch came in early fall when a group of fifty people from Microsoft flew down to IBM's OS/2 headquarters in Boca Raton, Florida, and settled in for a month.

After two visits to England, with the Microsoft developers bailing out the IBMers, even Big Blue had realized that the situation was not ideal. To fix it, they moved a bunch of the Hursley developers to Boca for the duration of OS/2 PM. The developers from Microsoft again went down on a rescue mission, again bringing their own equipment, and they set up in the IBM cafeteria with half the English guys, working fifteen-hour days, after which they would repair to the luxuries of a Residence Inn.

Fellow Microsoftie Richard Tate was the official liaison who handled the politics with IBM. He was a marketing guy and was therefore assumed to be better equipped at sucking up and handling absurd bureaucracy.

Anytime someone broke IBM's rules, they received a security violation. Tate, for instance, had an answering machine, which like so many normal aspects of life, was against IBM's policy.

"Can't have that," the security guard said, slapping a violation on Tate's desk. Marketeer Tate proudly collected more little red flags that said "violation" than any of the developers.

If IBM security thought a desk was "safe" the flag would be green, but if it was unlocked, they would turn it over, posting a "violation" sign.

To relieve the stress of this Dilbert gulag, the Microsoft developers often played Nerf football in the hallway outside Tate's office. One time a developer threw the ball a little high, and it clipped the smoke detector, setting off the alarm. Surprisingly, it took ten minutes for the security guy to arrive.

"Alarm just went off in here," the guard said. "Anything going on?"

"Nope, just working," Wood said.

While at IBM, Microsoft employees were not even allowed to go out in the hallway unless escorted by an IBM employee. Wood couldn't even walk to the bathroom without an IBMer tagging along.

At least fair-minded in their obsessiveness, IBM had another rule stating that if something was marked "Microsoft Confidential," then no IBM employee could touch it, not even security guards. No matter if they thought there was a bomb in it. If it said "Microsoft Confidential," IBM's attorneys had instructed its employees to keep their hands off.

Eventually one of the Microsoft developers bought a hot plate at a flea market and brought it in so everyone could have coffee without having to involve an escort.

The next day the security guard came by.

"Excuse me," he said. "It's IBM policy, and safety regulations say you can't have a hot plate in this room here. There's a hot plate down the hall, which has hot coffee. It's okay to have hot plates there, but not in this room here."

One of the Microsoft guys picked up a cardboard box, wrote "Microsoft Confidential" on it, and plopped it down over the steaming coffee on the operating hot plate.

"Good enough," the security guard said.

At IBM, confidentiality trumped fire code.

Joint development with IBM proved to be a recurring nightmare. Microsoft had its OS/2 group in Boca Raton writing software, and an OS/2 group in Redmond writing software, and communications were difficult at best. People from Microsoft headquarters had to be flown back and forth across the country to get anything done and checked into the system. IBM also had laboriously painful procedures for quality assurance.

Of course, Microsoft's public relations was telling the world that the work with IBM was proceeding beautifully, and OS/2 was right on schedule.

"We're not going to be late with this product," Microsoft's then president, Jon Shirley, said. "We've never announced a DOS and missed a date, and this is the biggest and best organized software project we've ever managed."

Meanwhile, the Microsoft OS/2 team was having problems getting even the most basic parts of the OS/2 code up and running. The biggest problem was the number of people a developer had to filter up through to get any design changed. At least at Microsoft, whether the design process worked or not, it had the virtue of simplicity.

At IBM, even before they began writing the software, they first created product specifications. Then those documents were frozen so that new features couldn't easily be added. Inevitably one of the Microsoft developers, who hadn't been part of the design process, would say, "If we did it this way it would be much better."

"We've already been through the design freeze milestone," IBM executives would reply. "Put that in the suggestion box for the next time."

Even on the Microsoft side, developers like Wood really didn't want to work with Microsoft's internal OS/2 group led by Gordon Letwin, so Wood often spent his time looking for things that Letwin's group wasn't doing right, and fighting to do things his own way.

Unlike Wood, Letwin had internalized Gates's desperation and signed on for anything IBM wanted to do on behalf of OS/2. Wood, on the other hand, thought OS/2 was a waste of time from day one.

On October 31, 1988, Microsoft and IBM rolled out OS/2 Presentation Manager, touting it as a giant step forward in personal computer software.

"This is the milestone that changes the rules for everybody," Gates said. "OS/2 Presentation Manager will be the environment for office computing in the 1990s."

No doubt about it, Gates and Ballmer were betting the farm. Still, in September 1986, while their fellow developers jumped on the OS/2 bandwagon, Dave Weise, Rao Remala, and Bob Gunderson stayed behind to attend to that ugly little Microsoft orphan, Windows.

The rationale for doing another version of Windows, Ballmer told them, was that Excel, Microsoft's first Windows application, needed a platform. But this would be the last waltz.

"This is it, after this we're not going to have any more Windows. It's all OS/2," Ballmer said.

Which was fine with the three developers. Anything was better than working with IBM.

The goal of Windows 2.0 was clear: Provide that platform for Excel, and oh yeah, while you're at it—make Windows look more like the Mac.

After a year of programming, on September 6, 1987, Microsoft shipped a version of Windows 386, also known as Windows 2.01, to

Houston-based Compaq Computer Corporation. Riddled with bugs, it was rushed out the door just in time for Compaq's big announcement a few days later. The Windows developers turned around and finished up version 2.02 in October, the version of Windows that supported Excel. In version 2.03, the team fixed even more bugs, before that version shipped on November 17, 1987.

Windows 2.03 rolled into the consumer marketplace in January 1988, where once again, like its predecessor, it was met with something less than open arms. Its one notable innovation was that the developers had changed the tiled windows to overlapping. This, of course, immediately caught the attention of Apple Computer, which filed suit against Microsoft, alleging that the overlapping windows and visual displays of Windows 2.03 infringed on Apple's copyrights. The suit would drag on for years, trailing off into a kind of "so what?" devolution. The court ultimately would rule in Microsoft's favor anyway.

A couple of people were left to maintain the Windows 2.0 code and fix any bugs reported, but the "glory days" of Windows, such as they were, appeared to be dead and gone. Last one out, turn off the lights.

6

. . . .

THE CLANDESTINE EFFORT

I don't know, Steve. That's your problem.
—*Bill Gates*

In June of 1988, Windows seemed poised for last rites. After IBM finally relented and gave Microsoft graphics for OS/2, Big Blue must have assumed they'd struck the death knell for the old standard. IBM had given Microsoft their graphics business—what would be the point in continuing with this . . . sideline? Windows limped along on life support, nursed by a skeleton crew of developers. Ballmer and Gates all but forgot about it, fully committed as they were to working jointly on OS/2 PM with IBM.

But not so for Dave Weise, part of the Windows crew left behind in 1986. An irreverent programmer who had first come to Microsoft in the DSR acquisition, he had been sent over to the OS/2 team, but after six months he had reached the limit of his endurance for Big Blue's bureaucracy.

Arguing that he might be able to breathe new life into Windows, Weise persuaded Peter Neupert, who headed up OS/2 PM, to let him come back to the now dormant group. Windows had no defined deadlines, no clear features, absolutely no future, and therefore, no distractions. Just the ticket for a guy who needed a break.

At this time, mid-1988, Microsoft upper management, at the urging of its partner, IBM, had repositioned Windows as nothing more than an interim development platform for OS/2 PM, which was now less than six months away from being released. Gates reasoned that developers could write their applications for Windows, and then port them to OS/2. But none of the third-party developers like Lotus or WordPerfect would even go that far. In their eyes, Windows was a still unproven platform receiving faint endorsement from its own maker while facing imminent death at the hands of IBM's OS/2.

Of course, this utter hopelessness meant that Weise, newly rejoined with the Windows team, had plenty of time on his hands to embark on a pet project.

Weise began to ponder how hard it would be to get Windows to run in protected mode. Once again, this was the problem of the animals in the zoo. With a protected-mode operating system, applications could be confined to a certain space in memory by fences erected and maintained by the operating system. Each application would be required to live in a given area, which kept them in good order even if more than one was accessed. The payoff was multitasking without crashing the entire system.

At the time, Windows, like DOS, could only run in real mode. Here the applications were not "caged." Running wild, an application could write its instructions into memory, where the operating system, or some other application, might be storing its own instruction sets, thus bringing down the system.

Even though the current generation of Intel microprocessors (80286) could run in protect mode, when the computer started up with DOS and then Windows, the processor would stay in real mode and continue running DOS. Unfortunately this constrained the system to the old Intel limit—a maximum one megabyte of memory. If Weise could convert Windows into protect mode, then Windows could multitask, and Windows-based applications could access a lot more memory, which is exactly what they needed.

The idea was nagging at him when he ran into Murray Sargent, a brilliant physics professor from the University of Arizona on contract at Microsoft for the summer. Microsoft had taken notice of Sargent and the Scroll Screen Tracer (SST) debugger he had created, which allowed developers to find flaws and errors in their programs. It was a piece of technology Microsoft wanted so that it could move its own languages debugger, called CodeView, into protected mode. Sargent's debugger took real-mode, or nonprotected, applications and emulated them into protected mode.

Initially Microsoft just wanted Sargent's debugger for DOS, but Microsoft then realized that if it was going to move to a protect-mode operating system, which it knew had implications for OS/2, then it first had to have its language tools running in protect mode.

In late 1987, Steve Ballmer was so eager to hire Sargent that he not only offered him a job, he threw in 25,000 stock options, ten times more than the standard Microsoft package deal.

Sargent, who enjoyed the perks and prestige of being a full professor at Arizona, turned down Ballmer's offer (at 1998 stock prices worth $71.1 million), but agreed to sell his debugger. He also agreed to spend the summer of 1988 in Redmond, moving Microsoft's own debugger into protect mode and training someone how to use it.

It was a Friday night in June 1988 when Sargent and Weise ran into each other at a party in the Seattle suburb of Bothell, where Microsoft was celebrating the opening of its new manufacturing plant. Sargent was well aware of the problems Windows faced. It was a slow, buggy memory hog, a characterization confirmed by its dismal failure in the marketplace. It didn't support DOS applications very well, and it did nothing to solve DOS's memory limitations.

Sargent lightheartedly began needling Weise about Windows and its flaws.

"Windows 286 is a joke," he told him. "You just added 64K to the high memory area, but Windows needs an awful lot more than 64K. It needs a major transfusion."

"You're absolutely right," Weise challenged. "Let's go do it."

He meant right then and there.

Caught up in his own enthusiasm, a frenzied Weise dragged Sargent away from the party and the two rushed over to the Microsoft campus.

Unbeknownst to Gates, Ballmer, or Phil Barret, the Windows manager, Weise decided to spend the next two weeks seeing how much of Windows he and Sargent could hack into protect mode. Using Sargent's debugger, he began single-stepping his way through hundreds of thousands of lines of code. The debugger allowed Weise to go through and emulate Windows code running in protect mode to see where it didn't work. This would be the key to eventually moving all of Windows over to protect mode.

What Weise, in all of his zealous enthusiasm, didn't seem to see, was that a Windows platform, revived by being moved into protect mode, could threaten not only the existence of OS/2, but also Microsoft's entire relationship with IBM.

In July of 1988, midway through Weise's secret mission, Ballmer invited Sargent out for a jog on a little trail through the woods near Microsoft. While Sargent didn't spill any details of Weise's plan, he tried to tempt Ballmer with the payoff in terms he thought the marketing executive could understand.

Just imagine if Microsoft could get Windows running in protect mode. DOS and Windows would run beautifully on existing 286 machines. OS/2, on the other hand, is a big behemoth operating system, which would never fit on a 286 machine, as IBM was proposing. Windows, by contrast, was small. If Microsoft could alleviate the memory constraints of Windows, Microsoft wouldn't have to junk all of the old DOS applications. It would be the miracle cure, the marriage of the old and the new, the best of all possible worlds.

"You know," Ballmer said. "That's what we wanted to do all along."

Ballmer and Gates had toyed with the idea, at some future

date, of putting the display drivers into protect mode to support Microsoft's emerging multimedia efforts, but it had never been clear when or if this would happen. Yet Gates and Ballmer had never talked about putting *all* of Windows into protect mode. They thought it would be too difficult. Moreover, there was the problem of competing with OS/2.

Sargent kept his mouth shut on the subject of Windows for the remainder of the run and for most of the summer.

Meanwhile, Weise worked nights and weekends on his pet project. By the summer of 1988, the potential ship dates and features for the next version of Windows were still ambiguous—a not uncommon situation at Microsoft, but with Windows the lack of strategy was particularly evident.

Developers at Microsoft held different theories about how much better the next version of Windows needed to be. Did Windows need to support more than just Microsoft's spreadsheet, Excel? What about Microsoft's word processor and a graphics presentation package?

The only definite benchmark facing Weise and the rest of the Windows team was a planning meeting tentatively scheduled for August, a session in which Gates would be brought in and possible new feature sets would be discussed. If Weise were going to go public, that's when he needed to have his new brainchild up and running.

Just three days before the big showdown, he took Ballmer aside to test the waters. If, after hearing the details, Ballmer still wanted to kill Windows, he could. Weise would gain the personal satisfaction of knowing and of having Ballmer know what he had accomplished, but that would be the end of it. No big brouhaha in front of Gates and Weise's peers.

Weise maintained a poker face as he explained to Ballmer what he had done.

"I'm this close," he said.

"Where is it at now?" Ballmer asked.

Weise didn't answer. Instead he begged off for a couple more days to finish his work. He arranged to meet with Ballmer the day of the big meeting—8:00 A.M.—to show him the Windows demo.

Weise stayed up until two in the morning putting on the finishing touches, then left the Windows system running before rushing home for a few hours' rest.

When he woke up, he realized he had overslept. He darted back to the office. Arriving a few minutes late, he discovered that his machine had crashed.

He went to Ballmer's office.

"Steve, did you see it?"

"Yeah, I crashed it," Ballmer said.

"It's not perfect, but it's running. The amazing thing is not only that the shell comes up, but all the desktop applications come up, and they all run."

Ballmer stared at Weise as all the implications settled into place.

"What do we do?" he said.

"That's up to you."

"We should bring this up with Bill. But the first thing you should do is probably tell Phil and Russ so they don't look bad at the meeting."

Weise gave Windows managers Phil Barret and Russ Werner a quick briefing. Then they congregated in the conference room with Gates, Ballmer, and the rest of the fifteen-person Windows team.

As the meeting began, the team members who were still in the dark began making suggestions about the features they thought should go into Windows. Ballmer sat in the corner smiling like a Cheshire cat. Then, in time, he interrupted with, "Bill . . . I think Dave has something to suggest."

Gates turned to Weise. "What do you have?"

"Well, I think basically we should run Windows in protect mode," Weise said. Then he paused. "And by the way . . . I have it running downstairs."

Weise jumped up and began sketching out the details of his work on the white board. The team members were gasping and blinking their eyes in wonder.

Gates listened intently as Weise described his progress. Then there was a long silence, a defining moment for the entire company. Here, dropped into their laps, was a protect-mode, graphics-based operating system, with a bevy of applications, and little or no competition.

Gates looked at Weise and said, "We should do it."

"What do we tell IBM?" Ballmer asked.

Gates hunched over and leaned toward Ballmer. "I don't know, Steve. That's your problem."

It would take another twenty-one months to ship the next version of Windows, dubbed 3.0. There were still major problems to fix, and the Windows team needed to make some concessions to OS/2. But memory, graphics, and speed were what people wanted—and now Windows had them all.

While Ballmer set out to tackle the *big* problem with Big Blue, the development team, reenergized by Gates's endorsement and a clear direction, went back to work.

People would be able to boot Windows 3.0 and then start a DOS application in its own protected-memory space. Running on a 386 chip, people could run DOS and Windows applications simultaneously. Windows had better memory management and crashed less.

When word finally leaked to IBM that Windows was running in protect mode, the men in blue suits flipped. But their anger was something Gates appeared not to understand. Even if there were now to be another version of Windows—one that would operate in a protect mode—Gates was *still* betting that OS/2, not Windows, was Microsoft's future. At least outwardly, Gates still described Windows as a placeholder until OS/2 hit the market. The only difference now was that the placeholder was a little bit better.

"The mind-set of Bill and Steve was OS/2 is more than simply memory," Weise explained. "OS/2 is a better operating system.

We'll get a little bit more success with Windows, but it certainly isn't going to harm the IBM relationship."

Windows 3.0 would give consumers more memory, and it could support multiple applications like Word and Excel. But OS/2 provided security and preemptive multitasking, which was what IBM's customers wanted. OS/2 would take over the world because it had IBM's name behind it.

IBM told Gates to kill the Windows project. At COMDEX, in November 1989, like commissars at a Moscow show trial, Microsoft stood up and pledged its allegiance to IBM.

"Microsoft would cease development of its Windows software after the 1991 release of Windows 3.0," an article in the *National Review* summarized. "Windows then would be left for the low end of the market, while IBM's OS/2 would become the main PC operating system for the 1990s."

Gates's statement was supposed to end developers' uncertainty as to which platform they should look to for their applications. Instead, it sparked the interest of the United States Federal Trade Commission (FTC).

While Gates still maintained that OS/2 was the operating system of the 1990s, Microsoft's own applications developers were caught in a squeeze. By the time Microsoft completed the OS/2 graphics deal with IBM, Microsoft's applications groups were already entrenched in their development for Windows. Gates told his developers they now had to move quickly to support OS/2.

The developers howled. They were almost finished with their Windows applications. When they were done, then they'd write for OS/2.

Thinking it would be easier to port a Windows application to OS/2 rather than starting over and writing one from scratch, Gates conceded.

The group finished up their Windows applications, but the fact that Excel, Word, and even PowerPoint, Microsoft's presentation application, were raring to go when Windows went out the door was simply a fluke. They didn't make any special use of protect mode on the first version, but they ran, and more important, so did all of the old DOS applications.

It was yet another instance of fate smiling on Microsoft, strengthening its dominance in the operating-systems business while opening a new door to increased market share in the applications arena. If it hadn't been for the serendipitous partnership of Weise and Sargent, though, Microsoft could have just as easily remained another small start-up, a slave to IBM. And the world would now be running OS/2 instead of Windows.

Windows 3.0 would thrust Microsoft, which at the time had only 10 percent market share on spreadsheets and 15 percent on word processors, to the forefront of the applications business. While competitors like Lotus and WordPerfect were chasing after the red herring of OS/2, Microsoft inadvertently found itself wrapping up new applications for the "Next Big Thing."

Many developers heard Ballmer say, perhaps in jest, but with a high degree of truth, "The real reason we wrote Windows is because we lost the applications market on DOS."

By 1995 Microsoft applications would capture over 60 percent of the stand-alone word processing and spreadsheet market. Weise and Sargent's work forever changed the evolution of growth at Microsoft. Over time it killed Lotus and WordPerfect. But most of all, it forever changed who was going to be eating whom at the very top of the food chain.

7

. . . .

BAD MARRIAGES END IN DIVORCE

Bill is very smart, but he's not Machiavellian.
—*Dave Weise*

On May 22, 1990, Windows 3.0 roared out the door an instant phenomenon, selling two million copies in the first six months. This was hardly what Gates and company had expected for their OS/2 placeholder, but son of a gun, it turned out to be just what consumers wanted. It simply took on a life of its own.

And so did Microsoft's stock. The company's shares rocketed higher over the next nineteen months, climbing 188 percent as sales of Windows 3.0 and Microsoft's new Windows-based applications soared. Calendar 1991 would become one of the strongest annual performances on record for Microsoft shares as they rose 121.8 percent in that twelve-month period alone. When the dust settled at the end of 1991, Wall Street would value Microsoft at over $20 billion, a gain in market value of 305 percent since the beginning of 1990.

For years, Microsoft had been allowed to go about its business. Windows 3.0 and its unprecedented success would change all of that, primarily because the federal government found the coincidental availability of three of Microsoft's own Windows applications—a word processor, spreadsheet, and presentation package—unusual, to say the least. Especially when all this development would have had to have taken place while the company was publicly backing OS/2.

Everyone close to the process knew what a fluke the Windows 3.0 success had been, but this is where Gates's strategically crafted public image came back to haunt him. Critics wouldn't buy that story. Microsoft's competitors believed that this was a strategic work of nefarious brilliance crafted by the geek-mastermind himself, Bill Gates.

This evil plan, as the critics saw it, was that Microsoft, all along, had only pretended to back OS/2, while it secretly worked on Windows and the Windows applications. This would jump-start their applications business, and then they would promptly abandon OS/2. In the meantime, competitors like Lotus and WordPerfect, which already owned the DOS applications market, would be left behind to play catch-up in the whole new ballgame—Windows. Consumers would have no choice but to adopt Microsoft's solution if they wanted a graphical user interface system *and* applications for PCs and clones. Microsoft would leapfrog from nowhere in the applications market to total world dominance.

The Federal Trade Commission thought the conspiracy theory held a lot more water than the fluke theory. Janet Steiger, elected chairwoman under President George Bush, was determined to revive her agency, which under the Reagan administration had fallen into a deep slumber.

In a policy statement in late 1989, James F. Rill, then the assistant general in charge of the antitrust division, admitted, "There is a growing public perception that antitrust has lost its purpose and potency."

Now it was time for the FTC to get tough again, and Microsoft was a great way to start flexing its muscles.

But first, the FTC needed to get approval from the Department of Justice. Anxiously awaiting the sanction, investigators began collecting news clippings to bone up on Microsoft and all the subtle complexities of the software industry.

In May of 1990, the DoJ gave the green light, freeing the FTC to open their probe. With no shortage of help from Microsoft's competitors, the FTC collected mounds of evidence showing that Microsoft and IBM had been in cahoots from the beginning. Through its investigation, the FTC deemed IBM guilty by association. Big Blue was no stranger to federal antitrust investigations, often having been scrutinized for the wielding of its vast powers. In the end, though, no action was taken against them.

The success of Windows 3.0 may have convinced the FTC that Microsoft and IBM had been conspiring together to make Windows—not OS/2—the predominant desktop operating system. But a new twist in September threw that theory into doubt.

IBM and Microsoft said they were recasting their relationship. Instead of jointly developing products, Microsoft would move on to develop a portable version of OS/2, dubbed OS/2 3.0 New Technology (NT). This new platform would run on processors other than Intel silicon, processors called reduced instruction set computing, or RISC, chips. Nonetheless, for its part, IBM would only develop OS/2 for the Intel platform. Under the new agreement, both IBM and Microsoft would be allowed to sell each other's operating system products—including Microsoft's Windows—until September 1993.

By November 1990, with the IBM-Microsoft marriage clearly on the rocks, the FTC's conspiracy theory was going the way of the "grassy knoll." The new findings let IBM wriggle free, but the FTC investigation of Microsoft would only intensify.

"Bill is very smart, but he's not Machiavellian," Dave Weise explained. "That's what happened when the [FTC and DoJ] came in to investigate all these allegations—they found out that most of them were simply bullshit. You look at the record of who moved over to the Windows group during the OS/2 project. . . . You look at all the E-mail that was sent up to the time after Windows 3.0 shipped. All it shows is we were behind OS/2 100 percent."

And Microsoft was. Throughout the 1980s, Gates's love affair with IBM was hot and heavy. Microsoft's entire company strategy was tied to OS/2, and Microsoft was not alone in this. Many third-party applications developers were betting the bank on Big Blue. Companies like Lotus weren't about to write for an unproved and unsuccessful platform like Windows, which had barely blipped on the radar screen.

In the spring of 1991, the Commission's probe, privately conducted, went public. When it did, the investigation gained momentum as more of Microsoft's competitors cried foul. The FTC expanded its investigation and began looking into whether Microsoft's own applications developers had unfair access to information about Microsoft's operating systems, access that gave them an undue advantage, and which in turn made it more difficult for competitors' software to run. The Commission, not to mention the competitors, wondered if Microsoft did in fact maintain that so-called Chinese Wall between their applications and operating-systems divisions.

And yet, the FTC's probe had little if any immediate impact on Microsoft or on the sales of Windows. By the end of 1991, the number of users had reached five million.

Ironically, as Steve Wood explained, it wasn't until Windows 3.0 sold a million copies that Gates decided the project was strategic. Until the first million copies shipped, the Windows group had always hung randomly off of someone's organizational chart. But now the tail that was wagging the dog could no longer go unnoticed. Gates lured Brad Silverberg over from archrival Borland International to head the Windows team.

In 1991, with the FTC still hot on Microsoft's trail, the next version of Windows (3.1) got under way. But even then, Windows was *still* viewed as a placeholder—no longer for OS/2, but for what many developers believed was Microsoft's own successor to the Windows operating system, the project code-named NT.

Lin Shaw, one of Microsoft's few high-ranking women developers, and one who had worked directly on Windows, confirmed this sentiment. "Windows was not the glamorous group to be in," she said. "Even after [the IBM divorce] that was clear. NT was the new glamorous operating system."

Dave Weise agreed. "We're [the Windows 3.1 team] just supposed to get some stuff out there to make NT successful. So again, we're strategic, but only in terms of making other projects successful."

Before Windows 3.0, the strategy for NT was anything but clear. In fact, the impetus to begin the NT project was not driven by any product strategy at all, but was born out of Gates's desire to hire one of the world's preeminent software architects, Dave Cutler, and by Ballmer's need to retain one of the company's own software legends, Steve Wood.

Like Dave Weise, Wood liked doing it his way, and he did not like working with the stiffs at IBM. By the time he finished the last of the OS/2 Presentation Manager project in 1988, he was completely fed up with OS/2, tired of holding the hands of IBMers and fixing their ratty code. He longed for the autonomy he had once enjoyed working on Windows 1.0, where the die-hard hacker was left to focus on what he loved most—coding.

"OS/2 is going nowhere," Wood told Ballmer. "Let me do my own thing."

Ballmer knew that working with IBM hadn't been a walk in the park for Wood, who likened IBM to the Great Satan. Ballmer assured Wood that, as soon as OS/2 PM was finished, he could do whatever he wanted.

Wood was less than convinced by Ballmer's assurances. Ballmer knew what he wanted and was very good at manipulating people in order to get it. But to his credit, Ballmer made no bones about his tactics. He was very frank with the developers. The IBM business was important. Anything Microsoft could do to keep the business with Big Blue, it would.

Still, Wood dreamed of building an operating system from the ground up, and now was his chance. He decided to take the risk.

Across town, over at Digital Equipment Corporation's western outpost, renowned operating systems author Dave Cutler was also looking for something new. Cutler was one of the original designers of DEC's VMS, a minicomputer operating system built for DEC's powerful VAX minicomputer. VAX computers running VMS made DEC a market sensation during the mid-1980s, moving Digital from obscurity into the number two position in the computer industry by 1987.

Cutler was a brilliant programmer, and also a very frustrated one—DEC had reportedly canceled three of Cutler's projects. Gates saw Cutler as one more programming legend who would be a valuable asset to Microsoft and its operating systems business.

But Cutler had other ideas. He didn't care about PCs, and he wasn't coming to Microsoft unless Gates guaranteed him he wouldn't have to work on any PC operating systems. Cutler had sharpened his chops on big, secure operating systems at DEC. What he wanted to do now was to build, essentially, a minicomputer operating system that was portable. This meant it could run not only on Intel processors, but on RISC chips as well. He also wanted to bring his own team of programmers with him.

Gates said fine. He was willing to do whatever it took to bring Cutler to Microsoft, even if it meant letting him create a whole new operating system—one that would lead Microsoft God knows where.

In October of 1988, humming to the tune of a reported one million Microsoft stock options, Cutler came on board with his team of DEC refugees in tow. Added to their number was a sole Microsoft orphan, Steve Wood.

Work began on what many developers argued would become Microsoft's most important asset for the twenty-first century. Initially, this brand-new operating system, designed from scratch, was called OS/2 3.0 New Technology—NT for short. For IBM's benefit, it was positioned as a far-out version of OS/2.

Along with his team of DEC programmers, Cutler brought with

him a systematic method of coding and the grim determination of a paratroop colonel on D day.

Cutler had set his sights on the computers of the future. He would father the next generation of operating system technology, a system that could scale from a single-processor desktop computer to large, multiprocessing enterprise computers. NT would be stable, robust, secure, and portable. It could run on many different classes of microprocessors, not just Intel's. NT would be not only an operating system, but a network operating system as well, which could manage communications on one machine or on multiple computers, juggling details such as who has access to the network, while also allocating resources. NT would be Microsoft's chance not just to enter, but to conquer the network server arena, a market in which Novell had become the dominant player.

The operating system Cutler had written at Digital became the architectural basis for NT. But the challenges for the team were still formidable. They were operating in a vacuum. As other Microsofties before them had complained, they had no strategic direction from Gates, whose main objective had been simply to hire Cutler. If letting Cutler build NT was what it took to get him, then cool—that's what it took.

But Nathan Myhrvold, professional visionary, took a more focused interest. He believed that NT represented Microsoft's hedge against an Intel failure—an event he believed to be imminent. Myhrvold's cosmological intellect saw something not just heretical but apocalyptic. He argued that RISC chips would take over the world, challenging Intel's very existence.

Intel's chips were based on an older but widely adopted technology called CISC, or complex instruction-set computing. In the CISC architecture, large sets of instructions are fed into the processor in clusters of related operations. A CISC-based processor must periodically look back and check to see that the clustered tasks are being executed in the proper sequence. This wastes time and processor cycles, slowing the chip down.

In contrast, the newer RISC, or reduced instruction-set computing, model uses smaller, simplified instruction sets that impose limits on the number of tasks contained in each instruction. The net effect is that RISC chips can process these smaller instruction sets without ever having to look back, making the chips blazingly fast. Furthermore, because the RISC architecture uses smaller and simpler instruction sets, RISC-based processors use simpler circuits that require fewer transistors, making them smaller, and thus cheaper to manufacture than their CISC counterparts.

In theory, the economics of RISC-based technology suggested that it would be only a matter of time before RISC chips, not CISC chips, would dominate the PC market. But the theory had one major flaw—it ignored the overwhelming market dominance of Intel's CISC-based processors, the beasts that powered the majority of installed PCs.

Myhrvold had gotten the RISC religion when he read a book on computer designs called *Computer Architecture, A Quantitative Approach,* by John Hennessy and Dave Patterson. Myhrvold was concerned that all of Microsoft's products ran only on Intel silicon, and thus Microsoft's future was directly tied to Intel's, and to Intel's continuing ability to dominate the PC industry with its X86, or CISC-based, architecture. He said as much in a confidential Microsoft report he wrote in the early 1990s called "Technology Shifts in the Operating Systems of the 1990s."

Myhrvold convinced Gates that Microsoft needed to be doing a portable operating system—one that would run on a broad spectrum of processors. So with Ballmerian intensity, Myhrvold was hammering on Gates, touting, "RISC, RISC, RISC."

RISC would span all areas of computing from small consumer gadgets, to the desktop, all the way up to monstrous multiprocessing mainframe-like servers. RISC chips were better, faster, cheaper to produce, and far superior to Intel's CISC, or X86, architecture. Furthermore, after reading Hennessy and Patterson, Myhrvold argued that Intel didn't know how to build multipurpose chips like the RISC vendors did.

As Myhrvold pondered in his 1990 report, "You cannot help but ask yourself how all of those designers of CISC computers could have been so stupid."

In a later memo he wrote, "Price and performance are both at such a premium that one could equally argue that we are crazy to think that we can compete with a tired, old, overpriced Intel processor. Another argument in favor of RISC is that we are going to have to do this sooner or later, so why not take the pain up front."

Microsoft supposedly was warm and cozy in bed with Intel, yet here was Myhrvold, making damning statements about the microprocessor giant.

NT would not only give Microsoft a hedge against Intel, and an Intel failure, it would also allow Microsoft to compete with UNIX, a multiuser, multitasking portable operating system popular in the technical workstation and server markets.

So this was how Microsoft justified working on NT, Windows, and OS/2, all at the same time: Windows was maintenance, OS/2 was the new operating system, and NT was the portable platform of the future.

As for IBM, Big Blue could just fold these ideas from the NT project into a future release of OS/2, also known as OS/2 3.0.

Dave Cutler shared Wood's contempt for IBM, and from the beginning, the NT team was plotting to divorce itself from Big Blue and the befuddled OS/2 project. As a concession to Gates and his beloved IBM, the team promised that NT would run OS/2 applications. However, they made sure that OS/2 was something they could jettison when the platform didn't succeed.

The core, the guts of the NT operating system had nothing to do with OS/2, except for some OS/2 file system semantics. These vestiges remained only because IBM machines would most likely be on the network, and NT would have to be compatible with the OS/2 servers. But other than that, OS/2 was this "bag on the side," as Wood called it, a bag of code they could just lop off.

The NT team also kept a close eye on the IBM-Microsoft relationship, waiting for any sign of vulnerability into which they could thrust their OS/2-independent Windows NT.

They didn't have to wait long.

The moment the NT team saw the divorce with IBM brewing they lopped off their OS/2 bag of code. On their own volition, they put together a proposal for Paul Maritz, the manager in charge of the OS/2 project at the time. The NT developers proposed that Microsoft dump IBM support, and instead change all of the APIs to a 32-bit Windows API set, later to be known as the Win32 API. Wood and Mark Lucovsky, one of Cutler's Digital-deserters, sat down and, together, they divvied up all of the existing 16-bit Windows APIs, expanding them out to 32 bits.

Wood met personally with Gates to push this strategy. Both Gates and Maritz agreed to the proposal, which marked the beginning of the end of the IBM relationship.

In January 1991, Lucovsky, who spearheaded the Windows API effort, assisted in the formal presentation that Microsoft gave to IBM. He was up explaining the new Win32 API set when the men in blue caught the drift. Lucovsky continued with his speech, ignoring the smoke coming out of the IBMers' ears.

IBM looked at NT's interface and said essentially, "Excuse me . . . but this is just Windows, you didn't preserve a thing of OS/2 PM."

The divorce papers had been filed; the Microsoft-IBM marriage was about to unravel completely.

The change in strategy from OS/2 to Windows cost the NT team two years of development. All along they had wanted nothing to do with OS/2. Having been forced to expand the 16-bit Windows APIs out to 32 bits, then hack it to death, they would have much preferred to write new 32-bit Windows APIs from scratch.

After the divorce with IBM, suddenly there was intense pressure to deliver a version of NT. Having abandoned OS/2, Microsoft needed a network server story, and they needed it quick.

According to Steve Wood, "The divorce didn't happen with IBM until Windows 3.0 shipped and was successful and Bill said, 'Golly, gee . . . we don't need IBM. Oh, now we know our strategy.' "

The NT team's wasted two years was not the only cost of this sudden turn. When Microsoft decided to ditch OS/2, it damaged its LAN Manager networking product strategy as well as its languages business, both of which were based on OS/2.

What Microsoft lost in language and networking software represented additional years of work. It also opened the door for Philippe Kahn, a boisterous and outspoken competitor, to take his languages company, Borland, to new heights. Meanwhile, Novell Inc., based in Provo, Utah, continued to expand its leadership in the networking software market.

"We lost years of time in networking because of that abandoning OS/2," said Dave Weise. "We got hurt along with everyone else. Hell, the big story that this was all planned and blah blah blah . . . it's wrong. We had this Windows thing, but it wasn't meant to be successful."

Eller concurred. He had worked on the second version of the LAN Manager networking software after returning from Japan in late 1988, and he knew all too well the fallout from the IBM explosion that had drifted down on Microsoft's network group.

Eller had been responsible for the DOS component of LAN Man, which would allow DOS-based PCs to connect over a LAN (local area network) to OS/2 servers. A local area network consists of several PC users connected to a more powerful computer generally referred to as a server. Microsoft assumed there would be a transition phase during which corporations upgraded their DOS computers to OS/2, and both IBM and Microsoft wanted to make that transition as smooth as possible for their customers.

One of the problems Eller's group faced was that the OS/2 network components took up so much memory that DOS applications couldn't run on a DOS machine if it was connected to a LAN Man network.

Another problem with DOS LAN Man was that one of the work items added to the LAN Man team's list was to be compatible with Windows. Microsoft had finally decided it was going to ship Windows 3.0, so that needed network support too. And oh, by the way . . . Windows is going to be in protect mode instead of real mode like DOS.

So the LAN Man team not only had to support nonprotected DOS applications running on OS/2, it also had to support protect-mode Windows applications. This meant working jointly with the Windows team and the OS/2 team, which was no easy feat.

The overall perception of the outside world, and an opinion the FTC would later probe for underlying substance, was that internal Microsoft developers could easily get pieces of their code wedged into Windows, while outside software vendors could not. Microsoft developers such as Eller maintain that this perception was, for the most part, false. Windows developers didn't want additional work piled on them by Microsoft developers or anyone else.

It was a nightmare to get anything into Windows. Not impossible, just damn near.

With one exception, the internal Microsoft developers were in the same boat as developers on the outside. The only recourse unique to Eller and his buddies was that ultimately, with enough whining, they could get important issues ratcheted up to Gates.

Eller, who had worked on Windows 1.0, was well aware of the challenges the LAN Man team would face dealing with the Windows group, but he also knew from experience how to finesse the process.

"Have you looked at our proposal for how to fit in networking?" Eller asked at his first meeting with the Windows team.

"Don't need to," the team said. "We already worked it out with Novell. They're the market leaders. We work with their code."

"Yeah," Eller said. "But we have some problems fitting in with that model. We in the LAN group don't do things exactly the same way as Novell."

"Tough. LAN Man is piss ant. Novell owns the networking market, and we're going to support their standard in Windows. That crosses off the 'must do networks' check item for us. Anything else we can do for you?"

Eller knew he had to take what scraps he could get. "Okay, tell us how to do this. . . . I mean how does Novell do this?"

"They don't do that," the Windows guys said.

"Well. We need a way to do that."

"Hmm. That's a tough problem . . . but it's your problem not ours."

"Right," Eller said. "No question. But if you had to do that without changing a single line of Windows code, what would you do?"

With enough of this cajoling, over the course of a couple months, Eller and the LAN group figured out what they needed to do in order to work with the Windows group.

The Windows people had no idea how LAN Man worked, nor did they care, and no one on the DOS LAN Man team knew how Windows or anything else worked in protect mode. To make matters worse, the LAN Man developers, in keeping with their aggressive ship date, only scheduled one month to transform their product into something that would support Windows running in protect mode. Neither team could even think of a way that these two systems could be compatible, much less get to the point of worrying about who was going to be stuck doing all the work.

Eller knew his team was becoming delusional about scheduling. According to the schedule, they had four weeks to complete all work before freezing the code and shipping the product. They discussed several different approaches, then rejected all of them as unworkable.

Finally, inspiration struck, and Eller started hacking out his portion of the code, during which time he exchanged heated words with Andy Hill, the new manager of what Microsoft called the "Glue" group, the people who made the interface code that stitched all the major network components together.

"I have to have the whole thing done by Monday," Hill said. Then he asked Eller if he'd be working over the weekend to finish up his final piece of code.

"I don't work weekends anymore," Eller told him.

Hill then launched into the Steve Ballmer "Do you *really* believe?" lecture.

"I learned from Ballmer that you've got to have some spirit," Hill said, not realizing that Eller, having heard the speech many times, many years before, could recite the lines along with him. "You have to sign up for aggressive dates, then you have to bust your balls in order to hit the dates. And once you've signed up, your honor is on the line. You've got to do this."

"I didn't sign up for this stupid shit, and I'm not *going to* sign up for this stupid shit," Eller said. "This project is already late. And this project is going to be even later. You people are kidding yourselves if you think this is going to go out the door in August."

"No, man, we're committed," Hill said. "And if you'd get in there and actually pull on the oars, we could probably cross the line. It's people like you that are going to make us miss the ship date."

Why don't any of these bastards ever wear neckties? Eller stood there thinking. Then again, maybe his belt would do. Or maybe a blunt object.

The developer resisted his homicidal impulse and, instead, responded, "No, I don't think it's people like me that are going to miss this date," he said. "I told you what my schedule is. I told you I was going to have my stuff done by Wednesday. Not Monday,

Wednesday! I'm not coming in this weekend. The trouble with you, Andy, is you aren't willing to listen to schedules. When I tell you what the schedule is, you try to twist my arm to sign up to a schedule that I don't believe in. You learned that at the Steve Ballmer cheerleading school too, didn't you? Well, he's nuts, and so are you. I'm not going to do this."

"Boy, I'm sure glad you don't work for me," Hill said. "You are a hard case."

"The only reason I'm a hard case, Andy, is that I tell the truth. A concept some of you people don't seem to understand."

By this point, Eller was trying to figure out ways to get out of the networking group entirely, so he went to his boss, Ken Masden, and told him he wanted to move to another project.

"You have to get this one finished first," Masden said.

"No problem. I'd be happy to work on this until completion." Then, in a flash of inspiration, Eller asked, "But when is completion time?"

"We're going to ship in August."

Eller smiled.

"Fine," he said. "How about I stay until August. August twelfth, right? You won't need me after then because that's the date we're going to ship LAN Man."

"Right."

"Well then," Eller said. "I could sign up with another group and plan to move over on August twelfth. Of course they want to know when I'll be there, and I'd like to give them a time."

"Absolutely."

Eller knew he had a better chance of becoming a Victoria's Secret model than of shipping LAN Man 2.0 in August.

Quickly, he began looking around the company to see what other projects he could join.

Meanwhile, development on LAN Man dragged on for another year.

8

· ·

PEN ULTIMATE WARFARE

> We cannot hope to own it all, so instead we should try to
> create the largest possible market and insert ourselves as
> a small tax on that market.
>
> —*Nathan Myhrvold*

In August of 1989, Eller found a new home with his old boss Greg Whitten in the recently formed applications architecture group. Established partly to promote code and resource sharing between Microsoft's Word and Excel application groups, Whitten's team was also a reaction to a new software product from Hewlett-Packard called NewWave.

NewWave ran on top of Windows 2.03 and was part of HP's glowing vision of how the office of the future would work: orchestrated information sharing among different applications.

If HP were successful, it could end up owning the application programming interfaces, or APIs, dictating how applications would run on a PC. If HP succeeded, instead of writing to Microsoft's Windows APIs, developers might write to HP's. This was an immediate threat.

Nathan Myhrvold, sounding less like a cosmologist and more like some capitalist philosopher-king on acid, wrote of Microsoft's need to control APIs in order to maintain its stranglehold on the operating systems business:

The relationship of an application to the system APIs is similar to the relationship that the roots of a tree have with the ground—it is very complicated, and this makes it difficult for third parties to clone. This helps prevent competitors from dislodging a successful operating system. Evolution and innovation provide another barrier as well as upgrade revenue. The system must evolve its APIs and implementation over time in order to remain successful. This gives ISVs more features to exploit, makes it more difficult to clone, and it gives users a reason to pay for an upgrade.

The applications architecture group sprang forth immediately, and from it sprang object linking and embedding (OLE).

A method of allowing applications to communicate, OLE would produce another set of complicated software specifications that the software industry would have to support in order to be compatible with Windows and with other applications. Eller knew that because of this, Gates would view the applications architecture group as strategic. Hoping to avoid any more convoluted death marches, strategic is where Eller wanted to be.

The precursor to OLE was based on a technology called dynamic data exchange, or DDE, but it was very limiting. Regular DDE was viewed as a patch over a big hole in Windows 2.0. But it was just a patch; it didn't really cure the problem of creating data links and having applications communicate.

In the world of OLE, when an object, such as a chart, was created using a spreadsheet, the chart could be embedded later in a Word document. If any changes were made to the underlying spreadsheet, the update would automatically appear in both the chart and Word application.

Whitten decided that his group should design an integration layer, which could act as an intermediary between Windows and the applications. This would allow applications from any publisher to share data in a uniform manner.

The concept was great: Implementation would not be easy. Eller saw it as yet one more component that needed to be stuffed into Windows. The capabilities Whitten talked about for OLE spanned not only applications, but also networks and operating systems. The real problem would be to get all the groups inside Microsoft to agree on the specification, which was no small task.

Eller figured that since he was one of the only developers in the group with both systems (Windows) and networking experience, then he would be the great facilitator. If Eller could convince both the systems and networking groups to integrate a network dynamic data exchange, or netDDE, component into Windows, then the application architecture group would have the necessary foundation it needed to allow applications to communicate.

Eller first went to the Windows 3.0 group and met with Windows program manager Greg Lowney to see how receptive the team would be to inserting the necessary code, which Eller already had and knew to be workable.

Eller had stumbled upon a group of developers at Midland Bank in England who were using the regular DDE in Windows 2.0, slightly modified to run on a network.

The developers from Midland Bank said, "DDE is already there. We can use it for passing numbers around on one machine. Let's just take those same numbers, go down to the network BIOS, blow them out across the net, and let other Windows boxes use those same numbers."

These developers had written some code and had used it for exchanging data among different versions of Excel across their network. The Midland Bank developers had written the code, but their managers wouldn't let them use it because Microsoft didn't support it. Still, the developers were so eager for Microsoft to include the code in Windows that they offered to give it away free.

"Doesn't the code work?" Eller asked.

"No, it works great, we use it all the time. But we want to refine it and add some features. Then our management said, 'No way.

We'll support network DDE when Microsoft supports it.' They're worried that someday Microsoft will come out with its own network DDE, and then we'll have to change all our systems and conform to the way Microsoft does it."

Eller evaluated netDDE and decided that the Midland Bank code looked like a perfect solution. It didn't require any work, and the price was right.

"If the code works, great," Eller said. "We can probably use it."

Eller knew the problem wouldn't be with Midland's code, but within Microsoft. Namely, which group would own the code? The network group didn't want it—they figured it was related to applications or Windows. The Windows group argued it was an applications problem. The Excel group said it was a networking problem.

Microsoft could barely get the regular DDE into Windows 2.0, much less netDDE into Windows 3.0. It was a nice feature, but it involved applications, Windows, and networks.

Everybody's baby is nobody's baby.

The consensus came down that it was a Windows problem, but, as usual, the Windows 3.0 team didn't need any extra work—they just wanted to get their product shipped.

Eller spent the rest of his time essentially beating up on Greg Lowney: "Hey, you have to do this! You have to include this code in Windows! The world needs network DDE, and no one else will support it. The network group won't do it. The applications group won't do it. And besides, you don't want applications or networks dictating to you that this has to be in Windows."

Then, playing his trump card, Eller said, "You know our project is strategic. Whitten has Gates's stamp of approval."

Lowney caved.

"Does it work?" he asked.

"Yep, works great," Eller said. "I'll show you the demo. See, all you do is connect these machines up, and it works great.

Put this code in Windows along with the documentation . . . and ship it."

"Yeah, but we didn't develop this shit."

"Doesn't matter," Eller said. "Got to include it."

Eller continued to harangue Lowney day after day.

"So hey, is network DDE on the schedule yet?"

Eventually, just to get Eller off his back, Lowney committed to putting the code in Windows.

OLE, per se, wouldn't make its debut in Windows until 1992. It was heavily criticized for making the overall Windows system fat and bloated. OLE consumed memory, processor cycles, and, not surprisingly, was difficult for developers to support. Application compatibility introduced a whole other set of constraints on applications developers. But that was exactly what it was designed to do. As Eller argued, OLE was *supposed* to be fat and bloated. Integration was all about making monolithic applications slowly trade components among each other.

OLE was designed to protect the developers of big applications who were afraid of being scooped by slick applets, little applications being crafted by much smaller development companies.

Microsoft didn't want a lot of other companies writing code that could compete. It wanted to keep the barriers to entry very high. The idea, in fact, was to keep raising the bar, putting in more layers of software and APIs, which developers would then have to support. Microsoft wanted to make it so gnarly that anybody who couldn't devote a team of one hundred programmers to every Windows application would be out of the game.

Eller's stint in the applications architecture group would last but a few short months. As strategic as the group was to Chairman Bill, a new threat to the operating systems business had appeared on the horizon.

Now it was time to annihilate a new competitor, and Gates wanted Eller for the job.

• • •

In the fall of 1989, Microsoft was approached by a Silicon Valley start-up, two years old and funded by the best and brightest venture capital firms. Jerry Kaplan, chairman and cofounder of GO Corporation, wanted Microsoft to write applications for its new pen-computing machine. Jeff Raikes, Microsoft vice president and long-time employee in charge of applications, sent Lloyd Frink down to meet with them. Frink, a developer with a personality that mimicked Gates's, flew down to GO's headquarters and met with Kaplan and his partner Robert Carr.

Kaplan showed Frink GO's marketing and technical information. Frink thought the plans were interesting, but not compelling, mostly because GO still hadn't figured out whether it was building hardware, software, or both. Furthermore, GO was building its software from scratch, meaning it would not be compatible with any existing applications on the market, i.e., Windows. And the idea of Microsoft porting yet another version of Word and Excel to yet another random hardware platform that had no installed base seemed absurd. A much simpler solution, Frink concluded, would be for GO to run Windows on its new machine. Then all the existing Windows applications would work for GO.

"I thought he came here to build applications," Carr told Kaplan. "Not to convince us we're wrong."

A few weeks later Microsoft invited Carr up to give his presentation to the applications group, where he was met with the same response.

"All they did was beat me up about why we should be using Windows," Carr would later say. "They insinuated that if we didn't, they might do this themselves. After my presentation, they arranged a series of meetings to convince me, including several with key members of the Windows development team."

That was the last friendly encounter the two companies would have. Microsoft never arranged a follow-up meeting, and neither did GO. Of course, Microsoft had its own agenda.

By 1995, the pen-computing market was supposed to be a $3 billion cash cow. Millions of people from computerphobes to top executives would be using pens instead of a keyboard and/or mouse for inputting data. A glorified Etch-A-Sketch for the masses—only it never happened. Instead, venture capitalists poured millions into the pen-computing hype, which would prove to be one of the biggest $0 billion markets ever.

Eller's second daughter, Amanda, was born at this time, and when Eller returned from a week of informal "flex-time" paternity leave, Whitten pulled him into his office.

"Look at this E-mail," Whitten said, waving the printout. "You've got to go over and do this project."

The message was Eller's marching orders from Gates, tapping him to lead the Pen Windows project. During Frink's first forays into pen computers, he had tried to get Eller to come work with him. As a college student, Frink had worked summers at Microsoft and had spent time with Eller on some of the Windows 1.0 graphics. Eller declined the offer, but agreed to consult if and when Frink had questions. Pen computers needed handwriting-recognition algorithms, something that Eller, a mathematician, understood well. When Microsoft decided to officially set up the Pen Windows group, Frink told Gates that Eller was the man.

Eller left Whitten's office, stopping at the coffee cart in Building 5 before returning to his office. He set his latte on his desk and began writing a page-and-a-half response to Gates about pen computing. Eller said he wanted a year to explore the technology to determine what was technically feasible in the realm of handwriting recognition; he didn't want to commit to delivering a product when the team had no idea what it was going to build.

He shot the mail off to Gates.

Gates shot back a single-line message. "Sounds good."

With that, Eller joined the pen group as development lead and began recruiting. He even hired his dad, an electrical engineer, to work as a consultant on the handwriting-recognition part of the job.

By February 1990, Eller's group was partially staffed. They were already working on their first demo, and their mission was clear: Kill GO Corp. Raikes had said as much. Squashing the competition was not a written policy, but something woven into the ethos of Microsoft. Everyone knew that the company's bread and butter came from DOS, and, eventually, they would realize it would come from Windows. The abiding rule was to kill anyone trying to take that revenue away. The number one mission of Microsoft was to not let anyone else poach on its core asset—the operating systems business. And GO was looking like a serious threat.

Pen computing and handwriting-recognition systems had been done for over twenty-five years in Japan, but none of the companies manufacturing the systems ever made any noise. They weren't a threat. GO was. GO was trying to persuade the world that people needed its operating system, saying that neither Windows nor DOS provided the neat, new, cool functionality GO was promising. Without the GO challenge Microsoft may very well never have gone into pen computing. But now it was up to Eller and his team to go at GO and to take no prisoners.

One of group's first steps was to lay hands on a handwriting recognizer. Lloyd Frink purchased one from a two-man company called Infa. It wasn't great, but with practice, the software could recognize handwriting like a not particularly sharp fourth-grader. At least Eller's group was able to hack the software into Windows so that they could recognize text and use the pen instead of a mouse.

That summer, with a prototype pen machine in hand, Eller and his marketing guru, Pradeep Singh, headed for Japan to romance the Japanese hardware manufacturers. The Japanese always had been far more interested in handwriting than the Americans—kanji characters didn't have any convenient keyboard input. The Japanese also manufactured all the cool new consumer gadgets.

Singh lined up meetings with the likes of Sony, Toshiba, and NEC.

Eller donned the only suit he owned, and he and Singh showed up for their first meeting. Eller carried a Mitsukoshi shopping bag he'd picked up earlier that day at a department store. Everyone in Japan carried shopping bags—it was more appropriate than a brief-case. Eller sat down and fished the prototype out of the bag. It was a barely taped together Wacom tablet with an electronic drawing pad, wires hanging out of it, and power strips and cables—a typical engineering kluge.

Singh jumped into marketing mode while Eller booted the system. Eller then began handwriting on the tablet. The system barely worked, but as long as Eller wrote his letters in a particular way— he had practiced enough times so that the system usually recognized his script—it didn't crash.

"It's just a prototype," Eller explained politely.

The men nodded in unison as he demonstrated.

Then one of them asked, "May we try?"

He picked up the pen and attempted to write "hello."

"Wajeo" appeared on the screen.

Eller raised his eyebrows and smiled.

Fortunately, the executive assumed that the problem was his clumsiness at writing English. It must have been his fault the machine didn't recognize this writing. He never suspected that the software was totally wretched.

Many of the Japanese vendors had done their own experiments in handwriting, and they asked why Microsoft was promoting hand-writing recognition instead of keyboards.

"Keyboards are a lot better for inputting data," the Japanese said.

"Yes, that's absolutely correct," Eller replied. "But what's important about this device is not the handwriting, it's the mobility. You can take this anywhere, and you can make smaller machines because you don't need to hook the keyboard into it. That's what we think the real benefit of the pen computer is."

The Japanese were intrigued.

With each presentation, Eller and Singh refined their story. By the end of their weeklong trip, hitting two companies a day, Eller's handwriting was perfect Palmer System, and the machine never blinked. The demos went smoothly, and everything came off according to plan.

The trip to Japan had served its purpose. Now if the Japanese wanted to create pen-computing machines, they knew there would be no need to go to GO for the software—they could turn to their good buddies at Microsoft.

When Eller and Singh returned to Microsoft, they wanted to develop a kanji recognizer for the Japanese market, but the group didn't have time to write one.

Meanwhile Microsoft received a call from two businessmen who represented a Chinese developer, Xie Wei Dai (pronounced "Gee Way Die"), who had been working in his garage for several years and had written a kanji recognizer.

"You should look at it," they told Microsoft.

Microsoft flew these guys up to Redmond to see if the recognizer worked. Eller had searched the library to find everything Dai had published, including his thesis paper. When Dai interviewed with Eller and saw his own thesis paper lying on Eller's desk, he seemed convinced that Microsoft was the right place for him.

Afterward Eller and the program managers met with the businessmen in the conference room of Building 5. Dai, like most developers, looked as if he had bought his suit at a funeral parlor. But the focus was his recognizer, and when he demoed it, it looked pretty crisp.

"How much memory does it take?" Eller asked.

"Only a few K," Dai said.

"No way, you're kidding me," Eller's eyes bugged out of his head. "There's a few K in the kanji characters alone."

"Oh yes, it's very tight encoding, it's very good," Dai explained.

"Yeah, that's really godly," Eller said, wriggling the pen connected to the computer. "Let's try this again." Eller decided to show off and wrote the kanji characters for the day of the week. "Accuracy isn't bad, seems robust."

"Oh, you know how to write a Chinese character? Here, let me show you." Dai was impressed. "See, you can even write the characters in cursive style, and it still recognizes it."

Eller was flabbergasted. "You do both cursive and stroke-separated with one recognizer? That's *really* cool!"

Dai's businessmen were beaming. Microsoft appeared to be hooked. Eller and the rest of the group liked Dai's technology, so they began pitching him on Microsoft.

Dai turned toward Eller.

"This looks like a fun bunch of guys," Dai said. "I bet we could blend our technology together and do a good thing."

The two suits in the background, who were the CEO and CFO of Dai's newly formed corporation, smiled. As it turned out, they were the only two people *in* the corporation.

After several years building this recognizer in his garage, once the product was complete, Dai realized he didn't know how to sell it. So he went shopping—in the yellow pages, under "Suits," perhaps—looking for people who could help him build a company so he could sell his recognizer.

Naturally, the suits were happy to oblige. They filled out the forms to incorporate and voilà, they were family. The only step remaining was to sell Dai's technology.

The suits paraded Dai around to IBM, GO, and others hoping someone would step up to the counter and buy. But by the time they reached Microsoft, it was clear they didn't need to go much further.

When Microsoft asked where they valued their technology, however, things got sticky.

"Well there's an enormous market potential out there, so a couple million," one of the suits said. "Maybe three million. Something like that would be a good start—plus royalties."

No way, Eller thought. That wasn't the way Microsoft did business or bought companies. Microsoft generally paid a flat fee based on how long it would take its own developers to write the software. The lawyers took care of the details.

Microsoft's lawyers offered Xie Wei Dai $1 million.

"One million dollars—you're joking!" One of the suits laughed. "Get out of here! This is important technology. You're offending Xie Wei."

Microsoft didn't just want to buy the recognition code, they wanted to buy the guy who wrote it.

"Well that's fine," the suits piped in. "You can buy out the company."

"What do you expect out of this?" the lawyers asked.

"I think we should get a million dollars each for the whole company."

Nice thought, but it was Dai who had been working his butt off the last five years hacking out software on an old Commodore computer. The suits had just come on the scene in the last three months and walked Dai around to a bunch of meetings.

The lawyers counteroffered $100,000 per suit.

The suits replied, "Absolutely no way. We couldn't do anything like that. This is an enormous opportunity for you."

A couple days later, Microsoft's attorneys were talking with Dai in the conference room trying to draw up some agreement and settle on a price for the company. The two suits were telling Microsoft they wouldn't close for this and that, and then Dai happened to mention that he still owned the recognizer outright. He had a corporation, but he had yet to turn over the technology *to* the corporation.

The attorneys smelled blood. "Didn't you sign papers giving up all rights to your invention to your new company?"

"Well, of course," Dai said. "We made up papers, but I have not signed them yet."

The attorneys smiled.

"What does the company own?" they asked.

"Ummm, well, we have this paper of incorporation," Dai said.

"Xie Wei, how would you like to sell us your recognizer?"

"Well, I have these guys who helped me out," Dai said. "They were going to show me around and help me sell my stuff, and I don't really want to upset them."

"You won't be upsetting them, Xie Wei," the attorneys said. "We're going to pay them some money to buy them out. We think they should get something for their efforts. But you've been working at this for five years. You should get the lion's share. They shouldn't get the same amount. Why don't you talk to them, and see if you can't get them to come down to a reasonable price, and we'll try and do something."

Dai talked to the suits. Already nervous, they started raising questions as to whether Dai could even do the deal. Eventually, they turned around and sued him.

"All right," Microsoft's attorneys said. "Those sons of bitches want to play hardball, we'll show them how it's played in the big leagues."

Microsoft gave Dai a check for $100,000 and explained that this was called an "option." What Microsoft was buying was the right to purchase Dai's software and to employ him at Microsoft, if and when he could get rid of the suits. The moment he was free to negotiate, Microsoft would also give him a check for $1 million.

"Xie Wei, you have to get clear title to your recognizer," the lawyers explained. "We believe that the title is clear, but they have tangled you up in a lawsuit to make it appear unclear. It is our advice that you should spend some of that $100,000 to hire yourself a lawyer. We know a guy in Alaska who is one kick-butt attorney. We think you should call him up and offer to give some of that hundred thousand to shake those slime balls off your back. Here, we'll even dial his number for you."

The Microsoft attorney picked up the phone and brought in the Alaskan attorney. The kick-butt lawyer in Alaska promptly phoned the two suits.

"Ahh, I understand that you are harassing a client of mine with a needless lawsuit," he said. "We're going to sue you for encumbering his ability to sell code that he has a clear title to. First, we're going to sue you for that. Second, we're going to sue you for keeping him from getting a job that he would really like to have. I have a thing right here that says Microsoft is willing to pay this man a million dollars to go work for them and bring the recognizer. You are keeping my client from this legitimate income he could be making. It looks to me like a loss of about one million dollars. So, we throw a little harassment and irritation in here . . . seems to me like we can sue for damages of about five mil or so. So there's two lawsuits in your face. Think about that."

Then the lawyer hung up.

The suits panicked. They knew they didn't have any legal title to the recognizer, and they really didn't have much recourse but to drop their lawsuits.

"Hey look, this happens," the lawyer explained to Eller. "You go through a walk in the woods, and occasionally you get a few ticks in the coat of your dog. And what you have to do is go in there with a cigarette and just kind of burn the ticks out. That's what these slime-ball suits are, they're just a couple of ticks hanging onto Xie Wei's coat, and we'll just burn them out."

Within a month, Dai was working at Microsoft.

Not long after, another company came knocking on Microsoft's door. A group of Russian immigrants had formed a company called ParaGraph. Its chairman and CEO, Stepan Pachikov, was shopping its cursive handwriting-recognition software.

Gates, who had told Eller on a number of occasions that he longed to do a deal with the Russians because they were well educated and their labor was cheap, sat in on the meeting. In the conference room in Building 8 across from Gates's office, Pachikov demoed his cursive-recognition technology. It barely worked.

The pen group initially had attempted to do cursive recognition, but the results were equally unimpressive. The difficulty with cursive wasn't technology; the problem was that, when people wrote cursive, they wrote fast and loose. The computer had the same trouble reading cursive that humans did.

If Microsoft came out with a system that promised to recognize cursive, people would be disappointed. They would figure the system didn't work, and it would fail in the marketplace. However, if in its first version, Microsoft came out with a system that only promised to recognize print, people's expectations would be met. Cursive would come out later and be viewed as an advance on the old print recognizers instead of being branded a dog.

After the meeting with ParaGraph, Eller said, "I don't think we should buy their technology. Their recognition just isn't any better than what we already have. Their stuff really needs to be cleaned up. If we are going to spend the time cleaning up their stuff, we might as well clean up our own."

Microsoft held back, and several months later Eller saw the press announcement that Apple Computer had bought ParaGraph's cursive technology.

This was Eller's first indication of just how deep in the weeds Apple had shanked with its own pen technology, later to be known as Newton.

9

GO-ING DOWN

"We'd rather kill a competitor than grow the market?!?"
Those are clear lies.

—*Bill Gates*

In January 1991, at the Berklee Performance Center in Boston, GO Corp. announced a developer release of its Penpoint operating system. The moment that release hit, Microsoft turned up the heat on its own pen project, scheduling a February announcement for Pen Windows.

GO, which had no idea that the Microsoft steamroller was bearing down on them, had spent hundreds of thousands of dollars for its coming-out party. Eight hundred members of the Boston Computer Society showed up to see Jerry Kaplan and cofounder Robert Carr unveil a small tablet computer with a screen. On a stage more accustomed to Pat Metheny and Gary Burton, Kaplan proceeded to demonstrate GO's new system.

Meanwhile, sitting in the audience, deployed by Frink and Marlin Eller, was Microsoft's Wink Thorne. Playing it by the book, Thorne had even joined the Boston Computer Society the day before, then showed up for the performance, video camera in hand.

The next day, Thorne flew back to Redmond with the entire GO presentation on tape. Eller popped it in the VCR, and the entire group sat in the conference room like a football team watching game films.

At one point Carr drew a circle on the screen, and the audience gasped.

"Oh, listen to that audience respond," Eller said, smiling wickedly. "That's a killer. We've got to be able to do that. Do we have any code that can recognize that? No? How would you do that? Let me think . . ."

Eller wrote the code for that one trick on the spot. He conceived it in about five minutes, wrote it up in about an hour. Then his group spent the remainder of the month making sure they could demo everything the GO system had promised. They even added some features.

In his book about GO, Kaplan would offer his own theory of how Microsoft had skunked him. Little did he know—it was much worse, and much easier, than he'd ever imagined.

From early on, Eller and Frink had been arguing about the direction of Pen Windows. Most of the time the two resolved their disagreements, but while Eller had been off selling in Japan with Pradeep Singh, Frink convinced the programmers who reported to Eller to add new features that Eller had earlier vetoed. GO's marketing hype had corrupted Frink's imagination, and he wanted to include "gestures," easy ways of doing copy, paste, and delete.

When Eller returned he was furious to find his programmers busily trying to hack in gestures rather than working on the tasks he had assigned them.

"Read the org chart," Eller said, glaring. "I manage the programmers, not you. Your job is to convince me that maybe I should add features. If you can't convince me, it doesn't get coded."

"I can't convince you until I write the code," Frink said.

The gestures stayed.

Vice President Jeff Raikes, in his classic form, had organized Pen Windows just like every other applications group. He appointed

Eller as a development manager, Frink to be a program manager, and Pradeep Singh as the marketing lead. These three people all reported to a business unit manager, or BUM, who in the case of Pen Windows was Raikes. But he was never available to actually manage. Raikes certainly didn't have time to referee battles between Eller and Frink. By the fall of 1990, Raikes decided it was time for a neutral party to step in.

Greg Slyngstad, who had been group program manager of Word, was put in charge of the Pen Windows project, not because he had any familiarity with Windows, but because he had been the business manager for the entire Word group, and Raikes wanted someone in charge who he knew.

From that point, it was Eller and Slyngstad who fought all the time. Slyngstad told Eller what to do, but Eller didn't always listen. Instead, he would sit down with his people and kvetch about Slyngstad.

The real problem, Eller believed, was a typically fundamental flaw in management. Pen Windows was an operating system. It belonged in the systems group, not in the applications group. Naturally, Slyngstad, who came from applications-land, didn't see it that way.

For Eller, dealing with Slyngstad proved much more difficult than dealing with Frink. Slyngstad wanted to hire more program managers, and Eller had a complex and ambivalent relationship with program managers—he thought they were scum. As a rule, they joined Microsoft straight out of college, and their job was to write specs, but they didn't know jack shit.

In the applications group, PMs wrote specs and developers implemented them. This mentality emanated from Raikes, who years earlier had seen this system work beautifully on the Excel team. Program manager Jabe Blumenthal designed great product specs, Doug Klunder did brilliant coding, and all was sweetness and light.

But this was the exact opposite of how things ran in the systems division. Having grown up in systems-land, Eller knew no one followed specs. Furthermore, PMs didn't always know how to design code. Eller didn't see the point of wasting time writing a spec outlining that a save button should be drawn on the screen, when any programmer could put a button on a dialog box that said "save" quicker than a PM could type up a word document that said "put a save button on the top of the screen." No evidence had ever demonstrated that any product was superior because a PM had written a spec.

Eller expressed his displeasure to Slyngstad.

"You think some dream kid fresh out of school who has a degree in history is going to be better at putting the buttons on things than someone who's been hacking code for the last five years?"

"Yeah, quite frankly, yes," Slyngstad said.

Slyngstad assigned work to people according to their titles—made them learn to do the formal job description. Eller tended to divide tasks up according to people's talents. Good designers did the designing, good hackers wrote code. Eller didn't care what people's titles were, so he generally didn't hand out precise roles.

Slyngstad kept telling Eller, "Look, your job is code . . . and to see that your programmers are writing code. You figure out this handwriting stuff—that needs a mutant brain. We will use you to solve that hard problem, but we don't need your input about how to build a useable system."

Eller didn't like being told which problems he could solve and which ones he couldn't. The two continued to argue.

Eller had wanted to create an applet called Math Paper to demonstrate how pen computing was different from regular computing. Math Paper would do elaborate mathematical equations, and it would leverage the calculator that was already in Windows. Eller argued that by doing little applets, people could see where pen systems were especially useful. Eller's experience was honed from his Windows days. In Windows 1.0, the team designed Reversi, Color selectors, and a tiny word processor called Notepad—all crappy little applications, but they showed people what Windows could do.

When Eller suggested doing Math Paper, Slyngstad said, "No one knows math. You couldn't sell that. It's a niche market."

"Yeah, but it shows off what pens could do."

"Yeah," Slyngstad responded. "But we should be writing applications that will make us money."

"Yeah, but you can't make any money until you make the platform successful, and this is all about showing people how cool the platform is. We're not at the application development stage."

Slyngstad dismissed it, and that was that.

Six weeks after GO debuted its system in Boston, Microsoft held a big demo in Redmond to show Pen Windows to Microsoft's key hardware and software vendors as well as to members of the press. As far as Eller knew, there were no Wink Thornes out in the audience with video cameras—Microsoft didn't allow them.

Pen Windows was able to do everything that GO had done (no coincidence there), plus some. As an example of how the pen system would fit in with existing applications, they showed the calculator demo.

"We can do three-plus-four-equals-seven," Eller said. "However, this is a demo, and 'what you see is not what you get.' For once I'm going to open up the curtain and show you what really went on back there."

Eller showed the audience the method he used for doing the calculator trick. It was easy—he was using the old application that already existed in Windows.

"You write here," Eller explained. "You cut and paste the three-plus-four-equals into the calculator, then copy the results and paste them in after the equal sign. You reuse existing applications, rather than writing them from scratch."

And that was exactly the point Eller wanted to make—people would be better served if they went with Windows instead of going with GO because Windows existed. Developers could leverage existing Windows code, just as he had done when he wrote the calculator application in one afternoon.

The demo was a smash. Suddenly vendors and the press were expressing doubts about GO's Penpoint. Why reinvent the wheel when all you need is one more turn in the continuing evolution of Microsoft's ubiquitous windowing system?

But GO still had a number of champions, among them Esther Dyson, the highly influential industry guru who was scornful of Microsoft's ability to ever truly innovate. GO was her new passion, and Dyson touted their pen system, saying it would bring in a whole new class of PCs and computer users who were afraid of the keyboard.

Dyson argued that innovations in technology would come from small companies like GO, and since GO's system was object oriented, people could reuse the code. This was the revolution the world had been waiting for. GO was going to be the biggest Next Big Thing since the Mac had shipped in 1984. In fact, Dyson said that GO was going to be even more important than the Mac. GO's design was absolutely superior from the ground up.

Eller thought she was nuts. Why would people want to learn an entirely new operating system just to use a pen?

Microsoft public relations tried to do their usual damage control to counter Dyson's statements, but Eller figured what the hell—it was all free publicity.

Gates was listening, but he wasn't persuaded. He maintained that corporations who owned PCs would buy Microsoft's system rather than GO's. Like Eller, he felt people weren't going to want to go out and buy a whole new computer with new applications when a little extra software could be added to Windows and voilà, Pen Windows.

In early spring of 1991, Gates sat down for an update with Eller, Raikes, Slyngstad, and a handful of other developers. A half an hour into the meeting, Gates turned to Eller. "How do I know I've got the best handwriting-recognition system available? We're a rich company. I can buy what I want. How do I know I'm getting the best?"

The question was designed to rouse Eller and to challenge the troops, but after all these years Eller was inured to the technique.

"You're paying me to investigate handwriting technology," Eller calmly responded. "I'm giving you the report. If you don't think I'm doing a good job, get rid of me. You can read the research papers yourself. If you don't trust me, who do you trust? You can research the stuff yourself or you can have me do it."

"Well we should do *this*," Gates said, adding one more feature to the product's ever-growing list.

"Sure, we can do that," Eller said.

"I'm just not sure we're being smart about this."

"Well Bill, then I guess we'll have to get smarter."

• • •

Each year, Esther Dyson hosted an annual PC Forum conference for her closest friends, and for subscribers to her monthly Release 1.0 newsletter. The theme for 1991 was "Beyond the Desktop: Networks, Notepads and Legacies."

At a resort near Tucson, anticipation filled the corridors as people waited to see Microsoft and GO's dueling demos. Dyson walked on stage and introduced Jerry Kaplan, who repeated his "GO" show, last seen at the Berklee in Boston.

Then Dyson introduced the next act—direct from Redmond, Washington . . . *Microsoft's Lloyd Frink and Jeff Raikes!*

Gates sat watching from the audience.

Raikes led with the importance of continuing the investment in Windows, stressing that the world should not reinvent the wheel with some random new operating system that wasn't compatible with anything—not to mention the *über* application—

Windows. Frink then launched his demo. First he opened an application called Notebook, a little text applet, oddly enough, quite similar to GO's. Frink then showed exactly the same "gestures" that GO had shown. He drew sloppy triangles and other shapes on the screen, and immediately they perfected themselves with the tap of a pen.

As Kaplan would later muse in *Startup: A Silicon Valley Adventure*, it seemed to him that "Microsoft had used many of the same 'gestures' as Penpoint, but they were just different enough to avoid a copyright infringement suit."

There in Arizona, he and Carr sat fuming. They thought that Frink had stolen GO's ideas in 1989 when Frink first met with the company. The GO guys figured it had taken them years to develop their own Penpoint system—and here six weeks later those Microsoft bastards were showing the same thing. *They had to have stolen GO's sources! They had to have sneaked in and stolen information! That Frink guy must have told Microsoft everything GO was doing.*

Even if one knew about Wink Thorne and his furtive video recorder, it still didn't seem credible that Microsoft could have replicated the system in only six weeks.

"The reality is that we had a very flexible system, fast developers, and an operating system that was rock solid in comparison to what GO was developing," Eller said. "But most important, all we had to do for our demo was to replicate on our screen what they did on their screen. It wasn't like we had to build any real working code. We were just giving the impression of what we could do, just as they were giving an impression of what they could do someday. They did a demo, we focused on copying it as fast as we could. It took about four weeks."

During GO's presentation they had a canned statement from Jim Cannavino, a general manager at IBM, explaining how IBM was going to be making hardware for GO and running GO's software.

Microsoft had tried to convince IBM executives that they really didn't want to be tagging along with GO when they could be running Pen Windows. This of course went over like a chrome-plated fart.

IBM was still sticking voodoo needles in their Bill Gates doll for screwing them over with OS/2. IBM wasn't about to buy any damn Windows from any damn Microsoft, even if it did have pens.

Microsoft's strategy, nonetheless, helped sour relations between GO and IBM. IBM had climbed in bed with GO only to realize that backing GO's new operating system didn't quite jive with IBM's own OS/2 strategy. Big Blue started saying, "Wait a minute. Those Microsoft guys are not stupid. They're right. Why throw away a perfectly good operating system [and] have to buy a whole new one with a brand-new file system and brand-new buttons? Everything is totally different. We'd be contradicting ourselves and confusing our customers."

Then IBM got the grand notion that what they should have been doing was building pen extensions for OS/2. In the end, that's what IBM did. They abandoned GO's Penpoint operating system and went with their own Pen OS/2.

In the summer of 1991, Mike Maples wanted to demonstrate Pen Windows at Microsoft's company meeting. Eller decided that, while he was at it, he might as well show what object linking and embedding was all about.

Eller's group wanted Pen Windows to be one of the first supporters of OLE. OLE may have been a bag of dirt, but because Gates was excited about it, it was the only bag of dirt that was going to play in Redmond for the next couple of years. Eller assumed there were Brownie points in it for him to appease the chairman.

Eller lined up like a good corporate soldier, and it ended up costing him a lot of time. Eller didn't believe OLE had been designed properly. He figured he could demo what he thought OLE should be doing, rather than what it actually did. Then maybe he could shame the OLE team into doing something that the pen group wanted done, which was a feature called "edit in place."

Eller's group kluged up this demo for videotape that showed how edit in place would work. He launched Excel with a chart in it. Then he launched Word with the chart cut from the Excel program. The smaller Excel window was hiding in the background, and the Word window was bigger so the audience couldn't see Excel. Eller drew a gesture on the chart sitting in Word, which called Excel to the top. As long as Excel was in the right place, it came right up on top of where Word was, and it didn't look like anything had moved. It looked like Word had just popped up the Excel menus right into the middle of the Word documents so it could be edited. Eller made the changes in Excel and closed it. He hooked up a software instruction that told Excel to move to the background and disappear behind Word. Then it looked like he was working again in Word with the proper Excel document embedded in it.

It looked great on the tape, but it was total bull, pure smoke and mirrors, the apotheosis of vaporware. There was no linking or embedding occurring. Eller was simply pulling one application to the front of the other one.

At the company meeting, executive Mike Maples stepped up to the podium.

"Okay, here's this other thing we're working on," Maples said. "Here I have my document, and I have my tablet here." He held the pen up and waved it.

"Now I can go into my Word document here, and I can write."

While Maples was talking, charts and images flashed on the screen, and everybody thought he was actually writing on the pen tablet as he spoke at the podium. In actuality, he was just waving his pencil over blank paper while the videotape ran.

A year later they did the same demo, only this time it was for real. At a Microsoft party shortly thereafter, one of Eller's colleagues introduced Eller to another engineer.

"This is Marlin, he's the one who was the design lead on Pen Windows."

"Oh yeah, I saw that demo at the company meeting," the developer said. "That was really killer stuff. . . . But now that I think about it, I saw the same thing twelve months earlier. I mean it looks exactly the same. What have you been doing for the last year?"

Eller grinned from ear to ear. The only difference between the two demos was that the first one was smoke and the second one was working code—the true mark of demo excellence. The demo idea was to show what was possible. The trick was not to lie, but to be able to look into a crystal ball, guess what could be done and what could not be done, and then demo what could get done.

•   •   •

During the process of pen development, the political clashes between Slyngstad and Eller became so bad that Slyngstad wanted Eller out of the group. It was late December 1991, and they were six months away from shipping version one of Pen Windows. They were also beginning to work on the Japanese version.

"We're going to have to ship somebody off to Japan to start looking at the Japanese market," Slyngstad told Eller.

"Who were you thinking of sending?"

"We could send this one program manager," Slyngstad said, pausing for effect. "Or we could send you."

"I've been to Japan," Eller said. "I could do that. I wouldn't mind going back there. I'll check with the wife."

Eller went home that day and asked his wife, Mary, how she would feel about another six months overseas. Albeit a little miffed that Slyngstad was willing to ship him off just before the project rolled out, Eller was thrilled at the opportunity to go back to Japan.

He told Slyngstad it was a deal. Slyngstad was ecstatic, free at last from his bête noire in the black beret.

So Eller went to Japan, wife and daughters in tow, to work on kanji-recognition technology, and to once again try to convince the Japanese hardware manufacturers to develop for Windows 3.1, and to write applications for the pen extensions.

Some of the vendors signed up, as was evident on the Pen Windows press release, which said, in essence, "We have thirty prestigious vendors who are wholeheartedly committed solely to our product, and they say the future of their company's success is riding on our wonderful product."

As interpreted by Eller, what this actually meant was this:

"We've lined up thirty guys who are slick enough to put their names on a piece of paper and wave it around at the press saying Microsoft is going to be doing great things, and we're going to be right there with them."

The way this works is as follows:

Company A calls up Company B and says, "We're doing a press release. Are you in?"

Company B says, "Our name on it? Free advertising? Great, sign me up! By the way, what are you making?"

"Some stuff. You'll love it. It's going to be great."

But Microsoft wanted names like IBM on its press releases.

"Hey IBM, want to get up on stage with us?"

"No chance. We run our own PR, and we don't need to be tangled up in some stupid piece of shit you guys are doing."

"Cool. Maybe next time. Yo, Novell! It's you and me. You going to support this Microsoft stuff?"

"I don't think so."

"Okay. Catch you next time."

So for Pen Windows, Microsoft got primarily Japanese companies like NEC and Toshiba, a very telling statement about Microsoft's product and its political relationships. The best partners in the press release game were the Japanese, who didn't miss a trick, because they knew what the Pen Windows press release really meant.

"Oh, you need some face? No problem. Sign us up. Toshiba will be all over the technology."

"When?"

"Ahh," Toshiba said. "Soon, I'm sure."

It was a lot easier to line up companies like NEC and Toshiba because they were much more aware. They said they would support Pen Windows, but what they were really saying was that "should Pen Windows became popular, and should it look like a lucrative opportunity, they would most likely be there . . . someday."

When Eller returned from Japan, it was time for his annual review. He had been pushing to get promoted from a level 13, which was a group lead, up to a level 14, a cross-group lead. A 14, obviously, was one level below 15, which was a technical equivalent of a VP of the company. Only a handful of developers at Microsoft were 15s.

In the compensation plan Gates had created for his programmers, each programmer was ranked between a level 10 and a 15, with 15 being an architect—someone like a Jeff Raikes or a Greg Whitten. Gates said making it to a level 13 was like making partner. It usually meant more stock options. Making it to this level didn't require that a programmer perform management tasks—an innovative piece of software was enough.

So Eller looked at the other people who had been getting promoted to 14. They were his peers from the good old days. The description of what a developer needed to do to be a 14 was to work on cross-divisional projects, those that spanned both the applications and systems divisions. Pen Windows certainly fit that bill. It was classic cross-divisional work. Even before he had agreed to lead the pen project, Eller had discussed this issue with Raikes. By all rights the pen project should result in a level 14 promotion.

With Pen Windows shipped on time, and ready for Windows 3.1 to ship, Eller went in for the big tête-à-tête with Slyngstad, attired, as usual, in a T-shirt, jeans, and a black beret.

Slyngstad greeted Eller from behind his desk, chin slightly raised.

"I want a promotion," Eller said. "And I really need you to go to bat for me."

"Well . . ." Slyngstad said, clearing his throat. "I don't think you've actually done level 14 work."

Eller was stunned. "I wrote you a world-class handwriting recognizer, starting from scratch. The people from IBM . . . their research team admitted our recognizer is better than theirs. What more do you want?"

"You didn't stay until the ship date," Slyngstad said.

"What?"

"Well, you went off to Japan and didn't stay to see this thing through."

"You shipped me off to Japan because of the fights we were having."

"Well, see . . . that's another thing. We were fighting, and I don't think that's appropriate behavior for a level 14. So I can't recommend that you be promoted to that level. However, you know, I think we need a cursive recognizer, and I think if you'd sign on and do the cursive recognition, then that would be something we could promote you to a 14 for."

Eller simply got up and walked out the door. He would take it to Microsoft executive Mike Maples.

A couple days later Eller was sitting in Maples's double-sized corner office.

"I want to be promoted to a level 14," Eller explained.

"That's a noble ambition," Maples said. "But you have to understand, there are very few of those promotions. Gates himself does the promotions, and we only select like two people a year. So even if you're a great developer, there's almost no chance that you will get promoted. Also, in order to be promoted up to this level, you have to have a champion, someone who is the head of some major group, which means someone like a Paul Maritz or a Brad Silverberg. The real way that you get promoted is . . . You have to un-

derstand, a level 14 . . . regardless of what it says in the manual
. . . a level 14 is really an award that is given for sucking up. You
have to have a seriously brown nose in order to get to level 14. Now
if you want to know who you should be brownnosing, there's no
problem. You need to be sucking up to people like Maritz and Silverberg. If you like sucking up to them, they've got lots of crappy
jobs to do, and if you hang around and ask them, 'Hey, what crappy
job do you have for me to work on?' I'm sure they could give you
more work than you could shake a stick at. But you have to think
about it. Think about it from this standpoint. The project you were
working on was a very high profile, exciting job—Pen Windows.
You were darlings to the press, you were getting hot morale, you
had your pick, and everybody was clamoring to be in your group.
You could put together a team of studs. That's a fun job. Now,
consider the other jobs you could have. You could be working on
the next version of Word for Windows. A disgusting maintenance
job with no glamour at all. The people are unmotivated. The thing
is late. They all want to get off the project. You have no design
freedom to do anything because your design is all dictated by whatever random stuff the marketers tell you to do. The people are continually depressed. . . . Now that is a miserable stinking job.
Which of those projects would you rather work on? Well I think
there's no question. You'd rather work on the high-profile, exciting
jobs, rather than the disgusting projects. Well, that's what the level
14 is for—it's the reward we give to the people who agree to brown-
nose. If your goal in life is to become a level 14, I'm sure we can
arrange to find you miserable work. But I think life's too short to be
doing stupid shit like that. I think you've got a really excellent job,
and you should count your blessings."

It was an amazing speech. Maples had convinced Eller that he
would be happier standing still than he would be getting a promotion, which was a much nicer way of saying "Up yours" than Slyngstad's.

The last meeting Eller had with Slyngstad was actually rather pleasant. Eller went into Slyngstad's office after hours one day with a bottle of brandy and two snifters. They sat down to chat about how the project had gone.

Slyngstad said Pen Windows had been a disaster.

"What, are you kidding?" Eller said. "This was a success."

"You think you did a good job?"

"Yeah, I did a good job, you did a good job. We did a good project. This thing worked great."

"Well you know," Slyngstad said, "we haven't sold a whole lot of copies."

"Greg, look. This wasn't a thing about making money. This was all about 'Block that kick.' We were on the special team. We were preventing GO from running away with the market. That was our job.

"Look, your background is in applications, you have to ship the application. My job is in systems. Systems, for much longer on, has been completely 'Don't let anybody else steal DOS from us.' That's all we're doing. We weren't trying to sell software, we were trying to prevent other people from selling software.

"From my view, Pen Windows was a winner. We shut down GO. They spent $75 million pumping up this market, we spent four million shooting them down. They're toast. That company is dead. They won't sell their shit anymore. We did our job."

10

. . . .

MEET THE JETSONS

Remember this—that very little is needed to make
a happy life.

—*Marcus Aurelius*

Rippling water laps against the man-made seawall on the east-
ern shore of Lake Washington. Dozens of twin-engine Kobalt
speedboats, sailboats, and cruisers bobble back and forth, the waves
slapping against their bows. They are all lined up to see Seattle's
newest tourist attraction, perhaps even get a glimpse of the richest
man in the world should he don his swim trunks and climb onto his
boat to go waterskiing.

The sprawling abode of William Gates III is carved into the base
of a hillside, and it sports panoramic views of the Olympic Mountains. Virtually the entire front of the house is glass, trimmed with
natural wood. It looks like a modern version of a Pacific Northwest
hunting lodge, only on the scale of a corporate headquarters. In
fact, many developers said it was just that—an extension of the
Microsoft campus.

Gates's house boasts a sixty-foot pool with piped-in music under-
water, a sauna, two spas, a 1,700-square-foot guest house, a trampo-
line room, a twenty-seat theater, a twenty-car underground garage
that doubles as a basketball court, a one-hundred-foot pier from
which Gates can waterski, an arcade, a one-hundred-person recep-

tion hall, a racquetball/volleyball court, a million-dollar-plus care-taker's residence, and an annual property-tax bill of over $500,000.

Chez Gates, interestingly, is built to look as if it sits on two previous civilizations—the Stone Age, the concrete age, and then his house, representing the wood age. The design concept assumes that the Stone Age and the concrete age have both crumbled, with remnants scattered here and there around the property. For example, in the corner of the garage there is a hole big enough to fit maybe two cars. When people look inside the hole they see *old stone*—actually new stone made to look old as if it were from the Stone Age.

Get it?

Gates purchased old warehouses as a source of old-growth timber, and they bought a sawmill to recut the wood. He used the best pieces for himself, the second-grade timber left over he sold to friends, and the unsuitable pieces he scrapped.

Initially, Gates's house was designed as a bachelor pad, but when he decided to tie the knot with fellow (now former) Microsoftie Melinda French, she stepped in to make some changes. One of the first things she wanted to know was, "Where're the bedrooms for the nanny and the children?"

Instead of three bedrooms, there are now five.

Originally, the master bedroom suite had a bathroom so small that in order to close the door behind you, you had to turn sideways—this in a house budgeted at $60 million. But there are those who say the chairman ultimately spent over $100 million, because after the Gates's marriage, the house was essentially rebuilt, and nearly every change involved jack hammering down to the foundation and pouring new cement.

But while many billionaires might sport more tasteful luxuries, few can match the computing horsepower that Gates maintains, but the computers are not in the study, or in the basement—they are in the walls. These walls are about six feet thick, or rather there is a crawl space about five feet wide between the two sides of a "wall" that separates one room from another. This allows plenty of room to get in there to adjust the wiring, to embed TV screens in the wall, and so on.

Guests invited to Gates's house are given an electronic pin with a little sensor in it, which is monitored by the system. At the computer registry in the reception area, people log in their name and personal tastes, such as their preference in music and art. Scattered throughout the house are dozens of video projection screens, hidden speakers, and too-many-to-count sensors, which monitor everything from the lights, music, heating, and air-conditioning, to the security cameras mounted on the perimeter. All these features are supposed to help guests feel more at home . . . which leads us to wonder if Gates's friends grew up, perhaps, in expensive, high-tech penal colonies.

Nonetheless, as they walk to the bathroom, their favorite Monet might flash on the screen in front of them, and as they reach the rest room, the lights will turn on.

If it sounds like something out of the *Jetsons*, it is and it isn't. Definitely it's for the haves, and not for the have-nots. The technology is expensive—very expensive—largely because it isn't standardized. However, it could have been standard, far more accessible, and even relatively cheap, if only Gates had stayed on track with a pet project back in 1992.

Unlike many of Microsoft's projects, this one, named Homer—for software that controlled the home—was a giant step into the forefront of new technology. No other major companies were working seriously on it, and that was exactly the problem. Microsoft does best when it has a successful competitor it can copy and then crush. Absent someone else rushing such software to market, Gates simply let the project drop.

Homer began as Microsoft's first entree into the embedded systems market, software on tiny chips found in most every electronic device in the house, from microwaves to stereos. It was a potentially huge, untapped market. Homer's mission was to set a standard for controlling consumer devices electronically, through a single remote-control unit. This unit could do everything from switching the VCR to "Record" to lowering the temperature in the bedroom.

While most middle-class American homes aren't in the same league with Gates's, we do have our problems with electronic overload, exacerbated by having different remotes for each gadget. We often forget which functions are for what, and half the time we don't know how to operate the systems at all. Homer could have taken care of these problems and more.

Gates initially conceived of Homer when he visited the Japanese consumer-electronics giant Matsushita. When Gates returned from Japan, he asked his wizard-in-residence, Nathan Myhrvold, to dig up some technology Microsoft could use to work in partnership with Matsushita for home control.

One of Myhrvold's first stops was Greg Riker's office. Riker, a programmer with Microsoft since 1987, was fascinated by these kinds of gizmos. Riker had automated his own house, and Myhrvold went there for a tour.

In his bedroom, Riker had a 100-inch rear-projection screen built into the wall for video. He had about a half dozen other screens throughout the house, and any of the video sources could be displayed at any location. Riker, who spent ten years in the music industry before discovering computers, had four hundred CDs ranging from pop to rock, jazz to classical, arranged in several jukeboxes cabled together. This way, he could be anywhere in the house or outside and think, I must hear "Stairway to Heaven," and have it playing immediately. This also helped him generate thematic play lists for his dinner parties.

Throughout the house Riker installed motion, sound, temperature, and light sensors that he used to program various devices. The lights would go on automatically just as he woke up, the coffee would already be brewing.

Riker realized he could buy all these gadgets at Radio Shack and hook them together. But what was missing was an integrated system for connecting the toys.

In order to turn on the music from anywhere in his house, or to switch on the lights, Riker needed a remote-control unit and an interface. The remote he used wasn't a PC but a one-pound, battery-operated, portable television set with a color LCD screen. The computer responding to the remote unit was elsewhere, and Riker was simply broadcasting the TV information off to the remote unit. To do this, Riker used a board for the PC that took the output of the computer monitor and displayed it on the TV screen, and bang—the Windows interface was on the television set.

He then used an infrared mouse, the "space mouse," as he called it. He waved it in the air and pointed it, which was all it took to control devices from across the room through the Windows interface.

Click on the mouse and a menu popped up on the TV screen asking if the air-conditioning was too high. Waving the space mouse, he could click one of the buttons on the menu and lower the temperature in the living room.

Using his remote, Riker could run other devices—the lights in the bedroom, the stereo in the den, or the security system. Of course it all should have been seamlessly integrated so people could simply plug in new gadgets, and they would communicate automatically. But like most demos, this was a kluge to show how cool the world could be at some point in the not-too-distant future.

Still, Myhrvold was sold. He asked Riker to lead the Homer group. Riker accepted, and immediately found himself strapped to the wheel of a miserable deadline.

In only a few weeks, Riker and Myhrvold had to show the home-control demonstration to Matsushita. The two futurists brainstormed. They extracted bits of technology from Riker's house and then added features like a video camera showing who was at the front door, and a bird's-eye view of the floor plan so the home owner could monitor lights and the status of various locations.

Riker's next challenge was to create a portable version of Homer for the trip to Japan. Pressed by the deadline, he assembled a makeshift strike force to turn the technology into a working demo. He begged and borrowed good programmers to help him. Riker brought the pizza, and the engineers worked sixteen hours or more a day, either at Riker's house or at the lab he had set up at Microsoft.

By the end of three weeks, the demo was ready, and Riker and Myhrvold headed to Japan. Matsushita was interested and wanted to pursue the concept. That didn't mean, however, that the Japanese consumer giant was ready to sign on the dotted line.

Each long, grueling trip to Japan built only slightly on the last one. Each time, both Matsushita and Microsoft got only a little more specific. But based on those visits and on the demo, Gates gave Riker approval to proceed.

Gates was very supportive, if only because Homer was already feeding ideas to the people who were building his luxury home on the lake.

Riker was now cleared to begin recruiting a team of developers to work full-time on the new project. He first talked to Marlin Eller, who was just coming off Pen Windows. Eller had a couple people with him, and they were looking for another project to sink their teeth into. Riker had approval for three new hires, so Eller and his buddies signed up, doubling the size of the team.

For some time, Eller had felt Microsoft was growing away from its historical roots. While Microsoft called the chip that sat inside people's desktops a microprocessor, the fact that vendors could now put 40MB of RAM on it, install a gigabyte hard drive, and run millions of operations a second, meant that it wasn't a micro. It was really a small mainframe.

The software Microsoft was writing—big, thrashing, multi-tasking, multiuser operating systems—was not the kind of business Eller had wanted to be in when he first joined the company in 1982. He'd had the opportunity to work at IBM and work on mainframe software, and he had passed. He wanted to work on micros where he could write tight code that fit into a mere 4K of memory, like the original Windows 1.0 concept. Windows had started out as a small operating system because the team was originally targeting an 8088 computer that had no hard drive, just two floppy disks.

IBM, on the other hand, was writing huge, monolithic software that ran on computers the size of Oldsmobiles. When the PC revolution hit, IBM couldn't possibly take its old mainframe software and put it onto a tiny little computer. But Microsoft could and did—vide Windows—and IBM missed that market. Microsoft didn't make the kind of margins that IBM made on its software, but Microsoft made up the difference in volume.

True microprocessors had moved into the microwave oven, the refrigerator, and fuel injectors. Tiny computers were now scattered throughout the house and throughout our automobiles. They just weren't called computers because they were little tiny embedded systems. And not one of these tiny systems used Microsoft software.

Many developers felt that Microsoft was now repeating IBM's evolutionary path toward dinosaurian sloth. Windows was so big and took up so much memory that it was of no use to anyone thinking tiny, embedded systems.

Inevitably, someone was going to own the embedded software market. Ideally, in the future, a PC would sit down in the basement next to the furnace or somewhere in the walls of the house. People would never need to touch that computer, nor would they need floppy disks for upgrades. In the same way heating ducts and electrical wires run throughout the house, fiber-optic cable would link the computer to everything in every room. If a new software system came out to improve functionality in the microwave or the CD player, that information would be automatically downloaded to the central PC via the cable.

Microprocessors would still be sitting inside the appliances, but they would simply run a single little operating system that would provide coherent communications back and forth. This way the PC could turn the lights on and off at various times, saving power, and the PC could make sure the oven was never accidentally left on. Instead of having twelve different interfaces in the home, one for the stereo, one for the microwave, one for the VCR, there would be only one: a Microsoft interface—like Windows.

Microsoft had already created this kind of dominance once, creating in Windows a virtual layer that hundreds of PC-related vendors supported. The consumer-electronics market represented a similar opportunity, except that it was a trillion-dollar business— ten times the size of the PC market.

Using a standard Windows interface, or even a speech recognizer, people could walk up to their microwave, regardless of the brand, and say, "Cook the chicken in ten minutes."

A button-lapel microphone or a remote-control device would send the command down to the computer in the basement, which would be a powerful multiprocessor Pentium machine that ripped apart people's speech and understood whatever was being said. It would then upload the microwave module: "Cook chicken."

In ten minutes, dinner's ready.

No longer would people have to worry about reading the VCR manual just to set the clock. Instead they'd tell the VCR to set the clock, and *it* would do it.

Eller's task when he joined the group was to investigate how all these electronic devices were going to communicate.

At the time, in 1992, several manufacturers, including Philips and Sony, were designing communications architectures such as the CE bus. Other companies promoted different architectures, each hoping to establish the industry standard.

Given Microsoft's market clout, whichever system it supported would *become* the standard, and then Microsoft would own that market too.

The Homer team met at the Salish Lodge in Snoqualmie Falls, Washington, for an off-site, all-day meeting. Off-sites were the new thing at Microsoft, shortened versions of Gates's "think weeks," in which the chairman took off two weeks every year to simply brainstorm.

At Salish, the Homer team discussed every aspect of the project. They determined that the key to Homer's success lay in RIP, the remote information protocol that would seamlessly allow every device in the home to talk to every other device.

RIP was a plug-and-play architecture for consumer electronics. Any device added would be uniquely identifiable and could be controlled simply by plugging it in. People would want to have a remote interface protocol so that any new gizmo introduced could be monitored from anywhere. "Anywhere" might mean another room in the house or another city. So if there were a storm, people could dial their house over the Internet and ask their friendly neighbor, Homer, if the power was on or off.

In addition to RIP, Homer also included other components. The group knew that Microsoft's object-oriented programming language, Visual BASIC, or VB, could be hacked up to write applications to control household appliances. What Microsoft needed to do was persuade the Japanese consumer-electronic manufacturers to bundle Microsoft's software in its systems.

This wasn't going to happen overnight. When a consumer bought the first unit, how would Homer, being a PC running Microsoft software, drive the stereo purchased five years ago? Consumers would have to go through a transition period. Either they would have to upgrade every TV, CD player, and toaster in their home, or Microsoft would have to offer an infrared transmitter and broadcast information so that the devices could respond as if to a remote. That would require Microsoft's querying the stereo manufacturers to find out what signals it needed to send through the infrared chan-nels. Microsoft could then program the appropriate commands into its system. Microsoft would end up having to write drivers for every consumer machine out there, in the same way that Microsoft has written drivers for every piece of software and hardware on the market, to make sure they were compatible. Microsoft would then make recommendations to manufacturers for what they could do to make their systems more Homer-compatible in the future. The trick was for a consumer's old Panasonic CD player to work with a brand-new Sony TV.

No longer would people who had a Hughes digital satellite sys-tem, a four-year-old Mitsubishi TV, a brand-new stereo system, and a year-old VCR need to juggle four remotes in order to tape a movie. If Microsoft brokered a single communications standard, all the de-vices would speak the same language.

Microsoft continued to work over the Japanese manufacturers, who were interested, but also worried that the Homer box would be too expensive for mainstream consumers. The consumer price point was perceived to be under $500, ideally under $300. The unit also had to be a sealed box, which meant somehow developers had to figure out how they were going to handle updates without con-sumers having to buy or do anything special.

Microsoft faced another obstacle. Consumer-electronic compa-nies were used to a world in which people simply flipped a switch, and the product worked. Computers were known to crash.

So the real challenge, as Riker and Eller seeded the idea with the Japanese, was to find a way to migrate Microsoft's culture and mind-set toward a consumer-electronic way of thinking.

Meanwhile, the developers implemented the Homer project into Gates's guesthouse as phase 1. A key component was the display remote. It looked like a regular handheld remote except that it had a screen and was two-way rather than just one-way. Using it, Gates could sit and interrogate every device. He could control the lighting, heating, and air-conditioning; a selection of music, video sources, and security interfaces; he could look at various points around his property through the remote video cameras. Originally based on Microsoft's Visual BASIC, the program later had to be rewritten in C. The objective was a fairly lightweight scripting environment that had fast turnaround so that developers could easily develop interfaces.

• • •

All was going well. At long last, Microsoft actually seemed to be making small inroads into the multibillion-dollar consumer-electronics market. Then came the battle of the warlords.

Back in 1988, Rob Glaser, who oversaw multimedia and consumer devices, joined Microsoft and brought with him a scheduler called "Project." Eller decided to try it, but the application didn't work for scheduling software projects—it required putting in a start and end date, something every schoolchild now knows to be impossible for software development.

One day at lunch Eller ran into Steve Ballmer and former Microsoft president Jon Shirley. When Ballmer asked how Project worked, Eller told him it didn't. He couldn't use it. It was a crappy application.

Eller returned to his office and the phone rang.

"Can you come over and talk to me about this?" Glaser asked. Booming Ballmer had wasted no time passing along word that the application was a turkey.

Eller really didn't want to waste time. "Project isn't useful for my problem," he said evasively, "but I'm sure it works for your stuff."

Then Eller listened to Glaser's two-and-a-half-hour pitch about the virtues of Project. That was Eller's first encounter with the man.

Their paths rarely crossed after that until late 1992, when

Glaser's group began competing with Homer. Glaser's new project was called Modular Windows, a stripped-down version of Windows 3.1 embedded in read only memory, designed for devices that use televisions as a display. It was the next move toward the digital revolution, the "information super highway," and it played off Gates's famed "information at your fingertips" vision for a computer on every desktop. The idea once again was to create the standard for digital devices to exchange information with one another, and to "play" applications created for one device on the other. Modular Windows would be the "glue" to tie everything together—Windows for consumer electronics.

As was the case with so many projects at Microsoft, Modular Windows was a reaction to a competitor's product. This time the target was Philips CDI (CD Interactive), a CD gaming platform for the TV set. And, again, as was so often the case, Gates was sending out conflicting signals, creating two separate fiefdoms whose territory overlapped.

Both Modular Windows and Homer were going to sit on top of the TV. They would use the TV as a display device, and they would do things for consumers. Where the projects differed was in the things that they did. But because they both sat on top of the TV, obviously one could argue for the economy of having one box, not two. Glaser argued that he was already doing this TV-based project that would deliver interactive entertainment on CDs through the TV screen. Glaser said he was already dealing with customers for Modular Windows. His group had already done press releases and customer calls, they had work in progress, whereas nobody on the outside had ever heard of Homer, which led some developers to wonder if Glaser's press releases were, in fact, nothing more than his *own* preemptive strike.

Glaser complained to Gates that the Homer group, which was under Myhrvold, was talking to the Japanese consumer-electronics people.

"Those are *my* customers!" Glaser yelled. "They want to know who's in charge at Microsoft, and Nathan's getting out there and confusing things. Read the name tag—Rob Glaser, consumer vice president. That's my area, so I want that Homer group."

Gates agreed. The Homer group was informed that they were moving over to Glaser's organization. And that's when the shit hit the fan.

Riker, who had worked for Glaser before, would have none of it. "I'm not moving. Homer is my project, I started it up on my own volition," Riker said. "I would be happy to run this project, but this is what I want! I've worked for Mr. Glaser before and he is a bully. I don't want to be in his organization."

Riker complained that Glaser treated everyone—employees, competitors, partners—like pawns, and there was always the sense that he had a hidden agenda. Others agreed.

One Christmas a longtime developer was chatting with a senior vice president, when Glaser walked up.

Just making conversation, the other two asked Glaser, "So what are you doing for the holidays?"

"Oh, we're going to go off to the Galápagos," Glaser told them.

The developer thought about those islands for a moment, famous for their role in the study of evolution's lower rungs. "Visiting relatives?" he asked.

Riker's threat that he would quit before he worked for Glaser worked for him, but Gates instructed the rest of the group to pack their things. Eller didn't see any reason why he should have to go over to Glaser's group if Riker didn't have to, and he balked too.

In the end, Glaser got the Homer project, but none of the people. No one was willing to work for him.

Soon after, Glaser received what was officially called an indefinite leave of absence, and the 150 to 200 people reporting to him all shifted over into Myhrvold's division.

Inspired by Glaser's departure, one of the engineers in his group sent around a little "Video for Windows" clip that they'd put together. It was a smiling picture of Glaser morphing into Myhrvold's smiling face. The rock melody in the background was "It's the End of the World as We Know It, but I Feel Fine."

Riker refused to give up on creating an affordable Homer device, but now it too had morphed. The new vision was called Otto, and it was software for the automobile. He took a demo down to a hackers' conference in Los Angeles and showed off his new baby.

Otto, which Riker put together in 1992, had a Global Positioning System (GPS) receiver, which is a serial port device that outputs latitude and longitude. That information was then fed to a map via a very small 386-based computer, all mounted in a motor home. The display from the PC was routed to a 19-inch television screen, which sat between the driver and copilot's seat. As Riker drove, he could glance over at the TV and see his present location displayed on the map.

The mapping software came from Automap, a company Microsoft now owns. Riker had only to write some glue code that took the GPS receiver output and transmitted the information to the map, which would reposition itself every couple of seconds, moving with him as he drove.

If he had a particular route planned for the day, Riker could see how far he was from his destination. He could also see if he was coming up on a big city and could summon up the coordinates of interesting places he wanted to see. Riker could also plug in his address book, which then might tell him that one of his friends lived twenty miles away and guide him through the detour if he wanted to go visit.

By 1995, Riker had a new version of Otto and a new RV. He took a year's leave of absence from Microsoft so that he, his wife, and their cat, Cleo, could drive across country. During his leave, Riker investigated both automotive computing as well as a wireless virtual office for Microsoft.

In his new version of the auto PC, Riker had a trackball attached to the steering wheel so he could navigate the map with his thumb. He kept in touch with the office using wireless E-mail, which was also new to the Otto software. In the future, Otto could even integrate speech-recognition technology, so when people plugged in a given route, Otto would respond by saying, "Turn right at Exit 505."

The Otto project was a lot like Homer in that Riker did it on his own. Both projects were in a gray zone in which Riker's personal interests intersected with a likely corporate direction. That was Riker's forte anyway. He thought up new ideas that might be fun to pursue, then got others in the company jazzed up about them.

When Riker returned from his sabbatical late in 1995 he proposed that Microsoft fund an auto PC project—which was quickly approved.

On January 8, 1998, Microsoft announced the auto PC at the Consumer Electronics Show in Las Vegas. The first wave of automobile manufacturers to adopt the technology included Nissan Motor Corporation and Volkswagen AG.

The auto industry was a logical market for Gates to tap—millions of cars, trucks, and vans sell each year—and the potential existed for a piece of Microsoft software to sit in every one.

The auto industry and the computer industry, Industrial Age and Information Age, Henry Ford and Bill Gates!

Now, that's what they call a grand convergence.

11

. . . .

HIGH ROAD TO MEMPHIS—
LOW ROAD TO MSN

Constant labor of one uniform kind destroys the intensity
and flow of a man's animal spirits.

—*Karl Marx*

In late 1992, the advanced consumer technology group was reorganized. Eller's low-bandwidth Internet strategy was dead. Gates would endure low bandwidth, per se, but it would not be Eller's peer-to-peer Internet model, it would be a clone of America On-Line's behemoth dial-up service.

But as usual, covering all their bases, Microsoft pursued a high-bandwidth strategy as well, one which would provide software and hardware for the emerging interactive TV market.

"It is extremely important that we have a strong strategy in each of these areas, for both the intrinsic merit and to meet these competitive threats," Myhrvold wrote.

At that point Eller had a choice. He could stay in the advanced technology group under vice president Craig Mundie and develop high-bandwidth technologies, or he could hitch his wagon to the AOL model of low bandwidth.

He didn't want to do either. He wanted to continue developing the downloadable language he had started in RIP, but he knew the idea would never fly. Myhrvold hated little interpreted languages, "intellectual AIDS," as he called them. The only reason Myhrvold had allowed Eller to design one in the first place was that the RIP group needed one. Now that RIP was resting in peace, Gates decided that Microsoft would be carved up along the lines of high bandwidth in Myhrvold's group and low bandwidth in Russ Siegelman's camp.

Still oblivious to the potential of the Internet, in May of 1993, Gates gave Siegelman, a marketer by trade, funding for a project code-named "Marvel." Marvel was designed as a proprietary network, a clone of America OnLine, where Microsoft could make scads of money on every transaction that took place on the network.

Eller didn't particularly like Siegelman's beliefs, which echoed Gates's, that a closed, on-line system, not the peer-to-peer, Internet-like model, would be the best solution for the dial-up, low-bandwidth world.

Eventually, Marvel would morph into the Microsoft Network (MSN), and it would end up competing *with* the Internet.

Gates had been inspired to fund Siegelman's Marvel/MSN project by two of Myhrvold's memos entitled "New Business Models for Wide Area Consumer Computing" and "Bootstrapping the On-line Information Business." The notion was that Microsoft needed to set up an on-line service and align itself with financial services companies and content providers to run a new system that would go well beyond AOL's and CompuServe's offerings.

The wide-area computing market was a huge business opportunity for Microsoft, Myhrvold opined in his September 8, 1992, memo. With wide-area consumer devices connected to a two-way communications network, such as the telephone or cable TV, consumers had to pay a fee to the network provider. Myhrvold expected to see a whole new generation of devices that would enormously increase the market, including smart telephones, interactive TV, and the expansion of on-line information services such as CompuServe or America OnLine. It was an area for Microsoft to exploit its four current business models: system software, horizontal application software, upgrades, and accessories such as mice. It was also another marketplace in which—no surprise—Microsoft could set and control standards.

"The people who can create the dominant format for consumer multimedia will be in an incredibly powerful position," Myhrvold wrote. "We should know, because we once upon a time exploited a very similar phenomena."

In order to bootstrap the market, and to control the industry standards for networked communications the way they had dominated the desktop with Windows, Microsoft would bundle the old remote information protocol with Windows. This would leverage both Windows 95, then code-named "Chicago," and Windows NT.

Giving the RIP software away on the PC was a peculiar idea for Microsoft, since it would remove a revenue source for the company, but Microsoft could recoup revenues by licensing the more expensive server software, which would run on Microsoft's NT servers. Microsoft could create and market the first server applications and provide electronic software distribution that would push hundreds of millions of dollars of products through its on-line network.

Once a service like this was established, Myhrvold said, it would be so lucrative that Microsoft could expect its on-line revenues to be many times more than its existing system-software revenues.

Myhrvold argued that Microsoft could leverage Windows, making it the ubiquitous platform for these on-lines services. Microsoft could also license the technology to other consumer platforms and convince hardware manufacturers to bundle and evangelize Microsoft's platform.

"The goal is that we would make this the number one way to connect to on-line services from Windows," Myhrvold wrote.

Microsoft would have a smart card, or some form of hardware, so that transactions could be handled securely. Microsoft would also provide, essentially, digital money via coupons or certificates. Then Microsoft could manage everything from frequent-flier miles to concert tickets. Myhrvold said that once smart telephones or other end nodes were commonplace, it would be easy for Microsoft to use the same system to start eating into traditional credit-card and cash-machine businesses. To pull this off, Microsoft needed to form a joint partnership with a financial services company that had the capacity to handle transaction and billing services, a company like Visa. Then Microsoft could cut itself in for a reasonably large piece of the business.

"Market presence and bravado," Myhrvold confidently wrote, "are enough to get us luncheons with nearly anybody, and we have been on that circuit for quite some time."

Microsoft needed to create proprietary tools to develop the on-line content and to use its leverage to establish good partnerships.

"Just roll up our sleeves and take out our checkbook and build a new group," Myhrvold said. "Because if you wait too long to start a new service you may find that somebody else who reuses existing information might get in ahead of you."

A month later, on October 12, Myhrvold defined his message again. "Our business model for extracting revenue from this sort of information world comes in two parts—how we make money from IIVs (independent information vendors, or content providers) and how we make money from end users," Myhrvold said.

In short, he concluded, "We cannot hope to own it all, so instead we should try to create the largest possible market and insert our-selves as a small tax on that market."

• • •

Wanting no part of Siegelman's low-bandwidth financial empire, Eller could either join the Video for Windows project, which en-abled people to play back, edit, and create digital video on Windows machines, or he could work on Myhrvold's pet project, science fiction video compression. Eller said the name "sci-fi" itself reflected what most people thought of the project. But Eller decided he'd rather be in on something from its inception, rather than join a nearly finished death march.

So Eller continued working on compression technologies with five of his old buddies from the RIP group, managed by an ex-naval officer turned developer named Paul Osborne.

Compression was essential, especially over a low-bandwidth network. It dramatically cut down the time it took to receive images over a network, allowing even the most impatient person to download most anything in a reasonable time. This would be important in the truly interactive world of the Internet where people downloaded not only data, but audio and video as well.

While Eller had earlier declined Osborne's offer to manage the Video for Windows project, he was still occasionally dragged into management meetings. For Eller, these were merely comic relief. For Osborne, they were his chance to strap himself into the Gates hot seat.

In one early meeting, Gates, ever the competitor, drilled Osborne about Apple Computer and its QuickTime video performance. Gates was not pleased about the performance numbers he had read in the press for Microsoft's own Video for Windows.

"But these are the numbers that my people ran off this afternoon," Osborne said, holding up his own stats. "And here are the values they got. I don't know where the press got their numbers."

"Why am I paying you people salaries?" Gates said, turning a deeper shade of purple. "Why don't I just go buy QuickTime?"

The situation worsened when Osborne explained to Gates that Microsoft needed to provide Video for Windows with support for MPEG 1, a standard compression algorithm for storing motion pictures.

"Fuck! It took you a year to figure that out!" Gates yelled. "Why didn't you do this a year ago? MPEG has been around that long. What have you been doing for the last year? If this is the direction we're going to go, we had a fucking MPEG encoder back from Tseng labs or whatever it was."

After the meeting, Osborne asked Eller if there was, perhaps, some more effective way to present ideas to Gates.

"Just go in and tell him," Eller said. "You could have said, well, Bill, we've been doing stuff. It doesn't change the fact that this is the direction we need to go. If you thought it was so damn important a year ago, you could have told us a year ago."

"No, no, you don't talk that way to your superior officers," Osborne said. "In fact, if you came in and said that to me I'd fire you for insubordination."

It seems Osborne's stint in the navy had been a graduate course in sucking up, but that was not the way to deal with Gates. Osborne walked away crushed and thought Gates hated everything he was doing. The Chairman Bill mystique was diminished for him; he concluded Gates was just mean-spirited.

Eller's group was preparing to present their science fiction image-compression demo. Mundie needed to see it, and Eller knew that if he wanted to schedule a meeting with Mundie, he had to set it up three months in advance.

Which was fine. The demo wouldn't be ready until then anyway.

Eller and his team worked day and night for the week leading up to the demo, and then the day of the meeting, Mundie sent Eller an E-mail.

"We can't make it to this thing, 'cause Bill has scheduled a meeting with me to do budgetary stuff at three-thirty."

Eller's demo was scheduled for 3:00 P.M. He couldn't understand why Mundie couldn't watch the presentation for at least a half hour.

Myhrvold, who was also supposed to attend the demo, sent an E-mail echoing Mundie's.

"Can't make it. We've got this meeting with Bill at three-thirty."

"When do we get to reschedule?" Eller asked.

"Well, you know the policy," the secretaries told Eller. "Three months in advance for Nathan and Craig."

Screw that, Eller thought. He'd talk to Gates's secretary.

"Hey, I had a meeting scheduled to demo some compression stuff at three P.M., and Nathan and Craig blew me off cause they have a meeting with Bill at three-thirty," Eller explained. "If Bill isn't doing anything from three to three-thirty, if he isn't scheduled, why doesn't he come over and look at the video. Then they can go right from the video into their budget meeting, get it started early, and everything will run crisp."

Gates's secretary put Eller on hold while she checked with the boss.

"Sure, that will work," the secretary said.

So Eller fired off E-mail to Mundie and Myhrvold.

"Hey dudes, Bill's coming to the meeting at three P.M., I think you should be there."

"I'll be there," Myhrvold E-mailed back.

Just before 3:00 P.M., Eller foolishly stopped by Myhrvold's office on the way over to pick up Gates.

Myhrvold jumped up.

"Fine," Myhrvold said. "I'll come with you." Eller had the distinct feeling that Myhrvold didn't want him to talk to Gates alone.

They picked up Gates at his office, and Myhrvold chitchatted with Gates about golf and other nonsense. Mundie was nowhere to be seen.

So 3:05 P.M. rolled around, and Gates was sitting at the table with Myhrvold, and Eller and his team stood around anxiously, ready to start.

"Well, we could wait a few minutes for Craig to get here," Eller suggested.

"No," Myhrvold said. "Let's just start."

Eller's team launched into their demo, and Eller grabbed Gates's arm and plopped him down in the chair in front of the screen.

"Get up closer," he said.

Gates watched, noncommittal. Then, later, Mundie showed up and stood in the back of the room.

Two days after the demo Gates sent around E-mail.

"We need to keep an eye on this technology," the message read.

Which scored at best as a neutral response from Gates, which was the kiss of death for resources.

Not long after, Paul Osborne told Eller that the entire Video for Windows group was moving back to the systems division— "Where we get to work on real projects, with real schedules that actually ship."

Eller's science fiction video compression, viewed as a skunk-works project, would not go over with them.

Eller found himself once more reporting to Mundie, who needed someone to manage all the core technologies necessary to deliver interactive TV. Mundie approached Eller, offering him the opportunity to manage the group.

"What are the core technologies?" Eller asked.

"Video compression," Mundie said.

"Cool. I buy that."

"Cryptology."

"I buy that," Eller said. "Encryption will be a critical technology for electronic commerce on-line."

"MMOSA," Mundie said. MMOSA was the research group's new multimedia operating system for set-top boxes.

"Total bullshit," Eller spouted. "That'll go down in flames."

"A new broadband network system," Mundie said.

"Down in flames too," Eller told him.

"We are trying to build a set-top box. Sort of an information highway PC that would sit on top of the television set," Mundie pressed. "It's Bill's vision."

"What's going to be in this set-top box?"

"We'll put a RISC chip in it along with some new graphics hardware."

"What kind of chip?"

"A RISC chip."

Mundie had long since gotten religion about RISC chips. Myhrvold, who didn't seem to care that Microsoft and Intel were thick as thieves, or that Microsoft's software and operating systems relied on Intel's chips, was the ultimate RISC evangelist. Myhrvold spread the gospel that RISC was going to take over the world. It was the better, faster, and cheaper solution. In fact, Myhrvold believed Intel would be left to wither on the vine as the world migrated to RISC.

Eller had heard these RISC arguments and thought they were absurd.

"And what fine software is this RISC chip going to run?" Eller asked.

"Well, we're going to write that software."

"So it isn't going to run Windows, right? Because Windows requires Intel silicon. And it isn't going to run NT either?"

"Oh, no way, NT is way too big. We're going to have to write our own windowing system from scratch to run on this system," Mundie said.

Eller was suddenly reminded of a similar conversation about a product ten years before. It was called Windows 1.0. What Mundie was talking about was building yet another version of Windows from the ground up. This was totally insane.

The goal now was to *leverage* the existing Windows, not to drive it into extinction.

But Mundie and Myhrvold forged ahead, anyway, reinventing the wheel, competing with the company's core asset with a new multimedia operating system called MMOSA. Rick Rashid, who had joined Microsoft from Carnegie Mellon in September of 1991 and was a director of Microsoft research, designed the kernel, which was now on a new RISC chip called Swallow. The actual prototype set-top box that software developers could use to start writing applications was called Penguin.

The better name would have been Turkey.

They were in a panic to release a competitive product to compete with the Philips CDI machine, which would allow people to run interactive CDs on TV. But Eller didn't believe the interactive TV market was going to happen any time soon. He figured it would take a minimum of five years, and it would grow out of the PC base. The MMOSA set-top box, on the other hand, was totally incompatible with the PC.

What Eller believed Microsoft should build was a high-end PC card that provided real-time TV and PC video, 3-D graphics, and high-quality audio. His argument was that people would use this technology on their PC first, and then it would migrate to the set-top box. While a PC card would be more expensive, the economics of volume inherent in the PC market would quickly drive down the price. Microsoft could then, one more time, leverage the Windows platform.

Eller kept his strategic advice to himself. He also rejected Mundie's offer to manage the core technologies team. So once again, he found himself reporting to yet another new Microsoft recruit, Will Wong, who was hired to manage the group and report directly to Rick Rashid.

After about a month Wong stopped by Eller's office.

"Let me buy you coffee," he said.

Eller and Wong walked down and grabbed a latte downstairs in the building.

"So you're one of these Microsoft millionaires," Wong said.

Eller nodded, stirring his coffee.

"What I want to know is why are you still here? Why are you hanging around? You've got sort of a reputation, and I'm trying to figure out where you are and what you're doing. Why are you over here on this little compression project? What are you people up to?"

Eller repeated all his woes about the recent reorgs and how his RIP group had been pulled away from him.

As for the latest developments, Eller said, "I predict the whole high-bandwidth RISC set-top box project Myhrvold's working on, along with all three hundred people, will go down in flames and collapse sometime in early 1995. I'm just laying low, waiting for the shit to hit the fan."

The problem, Eller said, was that Myhrvold had no respect for the installed base of PCs and was off making a lot of noise about things that had about as much basis in reality as commuter rail to Saturn. Maybe we should target Tacoma first, then as for Saturn . . .

"If I go in there today and tell the guys in the ACT group that their direction is totally screwed, they would tell me I wasn't with the program," Eller explained. "If I told the captain today the boat was sinking, I would just create a bad time for myself. Now if I wait till spring, when the water is up to the gunnels and rising, then I can say, 'Sir, I have located all of the leaks, I can plug them.' Furthermore, I think maybe we can limp into port. . . . I will be revered as a god."

Wong admitted that Microsoft looked pretty chaotic to him too. "I can't see any sense in the direction, but I'd always assumed that Microsoft knew what they were doing."

Eller laughed. "The only thing that saves their asses is that with $4 billion in the bank, you can afford to blow a couple hundred million getting things figured out in the early stages of a project."

With no confidence in what Myhrvold was doing, Eller took it upon himself to design a media board for the PC, with the ostensible purpose of running the video compression his team was developing. He dubbed it the Memphis Media card.

Memphis was the code name for one of the future versions of

Windows, something to be released after Windows 95. He knew Memphis Media was a name that would generate few questions and probably inspire neglect.

In truth, Eller wanted to keep people confused just long enough so that he could make sufficient progress to get funding from Gates.

Meanwhile, Eller had to avoid being killed by the MMOSA set-top box group. Until they got approval and funding from the top, the team couldn't do much—except have a lot of meetings. They met in the regular conference room for an hour or two every other day, discussing how they were going to present the Memphis project to Gates. There was constant pressure to cancel groups that sounded like they were merely duplicating someone else's effort, so the team schemed about how they were going to nuke the set-top box strategy. The most effort went into trying to show that their Memphis Media was *compatible* with Myhrvold's box. The principal product of the ACT group was creating slides, or "PowerPointware," demonstrating how any given group was, in fact, part of the set-top box strategy, even when it wasn't.

Eller's real strategy was to get the technology into the PC first, where it would then naturally migrate over to the set-top box. Eller argued that the media board would plug into a PC and essentially replace the VGA card, the video graphics array introduced by IBM in 1987. Microsoft could then own the new graphics standard. Memphis would have 3-D graphics accelerators on it so people could do things similar to what they could do on high-end workstation, but at a fraction of the cost. It would also provide video compression and decompression in hardware so that it could run full-screen sixty frames per second, which were standard, interlaced video signals used in TV broadcasting.

The Memphis name for a future version of Windows came from Microsoft executive and visionary Paul Maritz. This Intel veteran, a native of South Africa, discovered very early on that everybody at Microsoft usually described projects with a two-year event horizon.

Two years out was as far as anyone was willing to pin anything to a schedule. Maritz discovered that if he built his chart looking out three years, he could talk freely about the Grand Convergence and the merging of Microsoft's operating systems. At three years out, Maritz knew his solutions didn't have to be right—or even sound reasonable. Memphis just happened to be the latest iteration of this "Grand Convergence" scam.

By going under the Memphis aegis for his Media card, Eller could finesse the battle that was brewing over which group owned the graphics standard for the company. The systems division had traditionally owned graphics, but Myhrvold was building a totally new group to do graphics for the set-top box.

"How come Nathan's group is doing graphics?" the NT group in systems was asking.

Eller knew that, eventually, he would face the same question. But products never came out of ACT. When anyone questioned Eller's project, the Memphis name would make it smell like systems, not ACT.

When people asked Eller how his graphics-board project was going to coordinate with what systems was doing, he simply said he was coordinating with Memphis. And like Yossarian's liver pain that never quite became jaundice, that put the whole project far enough off in the future that the systems division would simply ignore it.

The problem now was coordinating this with the other random ACT projects. By this time, Memphis Media had expanded beyond the science fiction video-compression group that Eller ran. It now was a group of people—Will Wong, Dan Ling, Jim Kajiya, and others—all of whom were involved with graphics in the ACT group, and all of whom had problems with the set-top box. The set-top box was being designed for a price point that ruled out superior graphics, and it was already sandbagged by the ridiculously short time line that people had locked it into.

Eller quietly fanned the flames of dissension by encouraging them not to worry about the set-top box. "Take the time to design what you want to," he said. "Don't worry so much about the price point. Design a thousand-dollar card, not a hundred-dollar card. Microsoft always screws up its hardware designs by trying to build too cheap. Just make sure that what you design is the best and fits into a PC. That's what Bill wants. Trust me. I've worked with Bill. He cares about evolving the PC platform. This set-top box thing will die because it's not connected to the PC. If you tie yourself too closely to it, you'll just go down with it. Just claim that we are 'compatible' with the set-top strategy, that we're just the high-end version of it."

In early 1995, the Memphis group had another hour-long meeting with Gates to discuss graphics, one of the smoothest sessions Eller had ever seen. Gates's face didn't get red. He didn't pound the table. He was very subdued. He said mostly kind things about the project, asked a few questions that were quite sensible. The only piece of wrath that came out of any of it was not directed at Eller, but at Myhrvold, after he had left the meeting.

"This is what we want to have," Gates said, referring to the Memphis board. "Now, what I don't understand is why this fucking set-top box is supposed to be some goddamn RISC machine with some goddamn stupid non–PC graphics system in it. Explain the logic of that to me," Gates said.

But then he seemed to let them off the hook. "But that's for another meeting, on another day."

Perhaps Gates was mellowing out. It used to be that he seemed to relish raking people over the coals. In those days if Gates had wanted to pound down an issue, even though it was an argument with some third party not present, it wouldn't stop him from grabbing the nearest guy at the table and yelling at him with bugged eyes, "That idea is stupid!"

A few days later, though, news of the MMOSA project leaked to the press, and Gates approved funding for Memphis. Of course, life for Memphis meant death for the set-top box.

If Memphis was to be the survivor, then they needed to hire a manager to run it. Mundie, Rashid, and Wong each lobbied for his own people. Wong wanted Eller, Mundie wanted his buddy from another company, and Rashid thought his own friend should manage the product.

The loudest and most senior voice won the shouting match, and Mundie brought in a friend of his named Jay Torborg, who had worked at SuperMac, a now defunct hardware company in California.

Torborg was nervous about Eller, who at this point certainly was considered a dangerous unknown. Eller was an old-timer, and no one knew what his ties were to Gates. Torborg felt he needed to tread lightly until he ascertained just how much clout Eller actually had.

But by this time, Eller's options had vested. There was pleasure, even vindication, in the death of this MMOSA bullshit, and he began to think maybe it was time to ride off into the sunset with the "Sons of the Pioneers" hitting a high note.

· · ·

Being a thirteen-year veteran, Eller foolishly believed that Gates would personally handle his exit interview. He also assumed Gates would try to persuade him to stay.

He had heard that Gates was disappointed that so many of his old-time developers were leaving, and he blamed the fact on Microsoft's stock price being too high.

It's hard to keep 'em down on the farm at well over a hundred dollars a share.

So Eller gave some thought to what he wanted to do and what would entice him to stay. After much soul searching and jotting down of notes, he realized that, if Gates would give him a budget of one million dollars (i.e., about five guys for two years), and let him build his own project, he'd stay.

Eller had watched Gates squander hundreds of millions of dollars on turkeys like the set-top box, projects that had the smell of death all over them.

He didn't want a ton of cash, he already had that. After all, an option grant of, say, 2,500 shares was worth $52,500 the day Microsoft went public in 1986. At current market prices, and adjusting for stock splits, that same option grant was worth over $4.15 million. Money was not the issue. He just wanted to return to the environment he used to have at Microsoft.

But as Eller started making his list, he realized that his two most compelling demands would never fly. He wanted to choose his own project and be left alone for two years. He wanted to produce a product, and he didn't want anyone telling him what to do. Eller had already worked for people he viewed as ignorant and contemptible, and he saw no reason to prolong the exposure.

Gates had always been pretty good about letting someone bright haul off and try something different. But, as Eller quickly realized, Gates's generals and courtiers, the turf-warring VP weasels, would see it as a threat.

Bottom line, what Eller really wanted was autonomy, and he knew he would never again get that at Microsoft.

Some people like to use their talent and creativity to build things wonderful to behold; others simply want to be in charge. Sadly, as organizations grow, they fill out their ranks with the latter, and Microsoft was no exception. There were too many chains of command to deal with, too many fiefdoms to placate. Microsoft had become merely another . . . IBM.

One of Eller's comrades, Darryl Rubin, had a plaque on his desk that showed a picture of a little puckered anus. It said, "Unless you're the lead dog, the view is always the same."

Eller realized that working for the likes of Myhrvold and

Mundie, the view would be frightfully consistent until the end of the whole damn Iditarod.

Eller had witnessed an enormous transition at Microsoft. In the early days, people viewed the company as a development shop with neither clout nor credibility, but with a bunch of really smart and aggressive young programmers. Microsoft sold BASIC and other PC-based computing languages, and when Gates stood up and spouted his vision of computing, a lot of people laughed. Chairman Bill would stand up and say that Microsoft was going to throw the football one hundred yards down into the end zone, but companies weren't willing to go out for the pass. Well, after he completed a few "Hail Mary" touchdowns, companies began to listen. Eller felt like part of the original winning team, and it was fun. He and his comrades helped make Microsoft credible. The Windows 1.0 group had helped shape the future of computing.

Everything took on a different cast when Gates started hiring people from the outside, and putting them into VP slots, sometimes people who knew next to nothing about the PC industry.

A friend had told Eller that the reason Craig Mundie was hired was because he had worked at a super-computer company and had walked them through a bankruptcy. Gates had never been sure Microsoft would always be profitable, so he thought it was good to have people with diverse experiences, including failure.

Eller wasn't quite sure he saw the rationale of hiring a sea captain because he was used to crashing ships.

When Myhrvold found out that Eller was leaving he called him into his office for a chat.

The security door kerchunked behind him as Eller left Building 8. In the hallway, he had passed stacks of boxes piled floor to ceiling, remnants of the Fed's on again, off again investigation of Microsoft. He walked outside into Redmond's typically gloomy weather, which only intensified his mood. Eller set his coffee down for a moment and adjusted his black beret before walking across the Microsoft campus to Building 10.

The receptionist at the front lobby glanced at Eller's bearded face pictured on the employee badge draped around his neck. She smiled vaguely as he slid his card into the door. How "IBM" it was for an old-timer to have to pass through such tedious security measures.

Like Eller's, Myhrvold's office had a couch and was strewn with various books and white papers on computer science, physics, and math.

When he saw his guest, Myhrvold appeared concerned. Was Eller leaving because of him? Was Eller going to tell Gates about how screwed up the research group had become? After all, Myhrvold had seen Eller in the video-compression demo with Gates. It was Eller who had grabbed Gates's arm and plopped him down in front of the computer screen so he'd have a better view. Eller was the one who had called Gates directly when Myhrvold tried to bail out on the demo. Eller was a loose cannon, and worse yet, he might actually have some firepower.

Myhrvold seemed poised for doing some damage control. But in Eller's mind, Myhrvold was simply a political weasel, hardly worth the effort of maintaining animus.

"I hear you're quitting," Myhrvold said.

"That's right."

Eller stared at the bearded cosmologist, and in that moment decided it was time for a clean shave.

"I have a project of my own that I'm interested in starting," Eller said. "I want to run my own company. I've been here for thirteen years. . . . It's time to move on and do other things."

Myhrvold's face brightened.

"Good to hear that," he said. "Well, we're sorry to have you go." He hesitated, but only briefly.

"Well then I guess I couldn't talk you out of it?"

"No, I don't think you could," Eller said.

And that was the end of the discussion.

In August 1996, Microsoft announced its plans to enter the graphics arena and gave people a glimpse of the new Talisman, once known as Memphis technology. It was a reference design for hardware manufacturers, targeted at the high-end consumer market, which plugged into the PCI bus in the back of computers. Talisman was designed to replace a number of boards including graphics accelerators, 3-D, MPEG, video conferencing, sound, and modems.

The Talisman board was based on a chip from Samsung, and the first add-on cards were supposed to be available the first quarter of 1997.

Early on, Torborg had argued vehemently when Eller disputed the wonders of the Samsung chip. Eller had been pushing to use Texas Instruments chips, because they were already available on the market while Samsung's was just a spec. But Eller had been met with a deaf ear. Torborg said the new Samsung chips would handle multimedia much better than Intel's Pentium processor. Furthermore, they were much cheaper than the Texas Instrument chip.

Eller agreed that the Samsung chip would be the best solution— *if* Samsung could ever build it, but committing to Samsung meant banking Talisman's future on a mighty big unknown.

By 1997, the Talisman group had ballooned to over three hundred people. Eller, who had by then founded his own digital-music software company, called Sunhawk, kept in touch with some of his old buddies. Eller's friend on the Talisman team called him in late 1997 to tell him the news. Talisman had been reorged. Samsung had been late, then late again, and finally couldn't deliver the chips. And adding insult to injury, Microsoft had scared the hell out of its OEMs by saying that it was going to do a better job than they at building graphics hardware.

Eller wasn't surprised. He'd told the group from the beginning: Even if the Media card didn't ship, that didn't mean the project was a failure. The fact was that Microsoft had done what it needed to do—it had upgraded the PC platform. Microsoft had scared the OEMs into building better graphics cards. Microsoft could write new software for the boards, then consumers would be forced to buy all new hardware and software if they wanted the new killer graphics. Microsoft would make money, the OEMs would make money, the customers would get cooler games, it was all indirect as hell, and everyone was happy. It was business as usual for Microsoft.

12

. . . .

DODGING BULLETS

A lot of people make that analogy that competing with
Bill Gates is like playing hardball. I'd say it's more like a
knife fight.

—Gary Clow

B y the fall of 1992, allegations about Microsoft's "business as
usual" were coming up fast and furious. It was then that the
Federal Trade Commission decided to focus its investigation on the
issue of whether or not Microsoft's power and practices constituted
a monopoly.

Microsoft's case wasn't helped when two books, *Undocumented
Windows* and *Undocumented DOS*, written by Andrew Schulman,
appeared on the shelves. The books charged Microsoft with building secret interfaces into its operating systems, giving its own applications developers an advantage over its competitors by making
Microsoft's own applications run better than anyone else's.

Microsoft developers thought it was lunacy. The undocumented
APIs weren't published, they said, because they were APIs carrying
no guarantee of Microsoft support in future operating systems. If
outside developers used these APIs, their applications very likely
might not work on the next version of Windows.

Nefarious Microsoft became one of those urban legends like alli-
gators in the sewers: the idea that Microsoft had an applications

division and a systems division that supposedly had such close communications with each other and such great abiding love. It was ridiculous. But now prompted by the federal investigation, disgruntled competitors were coming out of the woodwork.

FTC investigators came into Microsoft and picked up boxes of E-mail and design notes off people's desks. Developers were not allowed to throw out papers, spec sheets, or other trash while the investigation continued.

By July 1993, the FTC itself deadlocked 2-2 on the question of whether to file a formal complaint. The fifth commissioner, Roscoe B. Starek III, who could have broken the deadlock, recused himself because of a conflict of interest.

Microsoft thought it was home free.

But Microsoft's rivals kept complaining. Justice, they said, had not been served. After three and a half years of investigating, in an unprecedented move, in August 1993, the FTC turned the case over to the Department of Justice.

Gates was infuriated. No other company had to put up with federal investigators going through their trash. It was reasonable for the FTC to investigate, but to have the DoJ looking into exactly the same issues seemed to Microsoft like double jeopardy.

But now the process began again. Employees at Microsoft couldn't throw out any documents. In Building 8, where Gates's office was, the hallways were lined floor to ceiling, for two corridors and wings, with file boxes full of papers collected for the DoJ.

It would take hundreds of people just to read through those papers. The DoJ estimated its investigation took 14,000 attorney hours, 5,500 paralegal hours, and 3,650 economist hours. The Justice Department received one million pages of documents, took twenty-two depositions, and interviewed more than one hundred people.

By May of 1994, Gates's patience was growing so thin that not even a public relations pro like Pam Edstrom could muzzle him.

On May 19, one of Edstrom's biggest nightmares unfolded on

national television. Gates had agreed to be interviewed by CBS's *Eye to Eye* host Connie Chung. Chung said she wouldn't ask Gates sensitive questions, particularly ones regarding the current Justice Department investigation. With that, "Gates's keeper" swung open the doors.

Gates was patient and accommodating during the interview, even when Chung asked him to jump over a chair from a standing position, a skill he demonstrated at various times, including once during COMDEX at the Shark's Club in Las Vegas in front of a packed crowd of admirers and computer junkies. So, once again, Gates complied, successfully jumping over a chair for the camera crew and their network TV audience.

But by then Connie and company had outstayed their welcome. Gates turned to Edstrom.

"Is this five minutes up? Pam, I mean, do you know five minutes?" he drilled.

Edstrom replied with a simple yes, but Chung continued with her questioning, drifting further and further off limits. She asked about his wife, Melinda. Then she brought up the STAC lawsuit.

In early 1993, STAC Electronics, which made data compression software, had sued Microsoft for patent violation, claiming Microsoft had used these patents in DOS 6.0. STAC said Microsoft had been in negotiations to license "Stacker," but talks disintegrated when Microsoft refused to pay the royalties STAC wanted. It was one of the only lawsuits Microsoft ever lost for patent infringement.

In preparation for her interview, Chung had talked to the CEO of STAC, Gary Clow, as well as other Gates rivals. She quoted a Clow comment to Gates on the air.

"A lot of people make that analogy that competing with Bill Gates is like playing hardball," she had Clow saying. "I'd say it's more like a knife fight."

"I've never heard any of these things," Gates said. "You know, you're saying like a knife fight. That's silliness. It's—childish. I mean, why be a mouthpiece for that kind of—of silliness? Why doesn't he just—just say them—anyway, it—because it has nothing to do with the patent lawsuit. It has to do with just, you know, creating a—you know, sort of a David versus Goliath thing out of it. Well, I'm done."

And with that, Gates walked off the set.

"Can I just ask you one more question, Bill?" Chung said.

His voice trailed off into the distance, "No, I don't think so."

It wasn't much later that Chung left CBS, and many people wondered if Gates had had something to do with it.

• • •

On July 15, 1994, less than two months after the infamous Gates interview, the DoJ and Microsoft finally reached a settlement via a consent decree, which amounted to what many observers said was little more than a slap on the wrist. The final judgment, or consent decree, filed in D.C.'s United States District Court, focused on two primary issues—product pricing and the bundling of other products with the operating system. In regard to bundling, the consent decree prohibited Microsoft from tying the sale of *separate* software products to sales of its DOS, Windows, Windows 95, or successor operating-system software, which the court defined as "covered product(s)." Specifically the decree stated that:

> Microsoft shall not enter into any License Agreement in which the terms of that agreement are expressly or implied conditioned upon: (i) the licensing of any other Covered Product, operating-system software product or other product (provided, however, that this provision in and of itself shall not be construed to prohibit Microsoft from developing integrated products); or (ii) the OEM not licensing piercing, using or distributing any non-Microsoft product.

In short, Microsoft was allowed to integrate new technology, but could not bundle other separate software packages with the covered products.

With regard to pricing, Microsoft agreed to change how it charged original equipment manufacturer customers who purchased its operating systems.

Under this consent decree, now Microsoft could only charge on a "per processor" or "per computer" basis—no more "lump sum pricing." Hardware vendors only had to pay for copies of DOS and Windows it actually shipped.

The agreement not only covered DOS and Windows but

> successor versions of or products marketed as replacements for the aforementioned products, whether or not such successor versions or replacement products could also be characterized as successor versions or replacement products of other Microsoft operating-system software products that are made available (a) as stand-alone products to OEMs pursuant to License Agreements, or (b) as unbundled products that perform operating system software functions now embodied in the products listed in subsections (i) through (v). The term "Covered Products" shall not include "Customized" versions of the aforementioned products developed by Microsoft; nor shall it apply to Windows NT Workstation and its successor versions, or Windows NT Advanced Server.

The court said that NT was not included in the consent decree because at the time NT didn't have a significant share of a relevant market. Little did the DoJ know that Gates would later be touting NT as the future of the company.

The consent decree also limited the amount of time hardware vendors were bound by Microsoft's licensing agreements. It also covered Microsoft's nondisclosure-agreement practices, which previously prevented software developers from writing software for competitive systems.

This was acceptable to Gates and to Microsoft's attorneys, all of whom were happy to put the past behind them. But the battle was not over yet.

At the September 29 hearing, U.S. District Judge Stanley Sporkin, who presided over the case, said that over the summer he had read *Hard Drive*, a book about Microsoft by James Wallace and Jim Erickson. Sporkin said he "thought it would be a good idea maybe to know as much about Microsoft as probably they're going to know about me." Sporkin proceeded to point out several allegations that were made in the book.

In particular, Sporkin focused on the claim that Microsoft engaged in "vaporware," which he described as "the public announcement of a computer product before it is ready for market for the sole purpose of causing consumers not to purchase a competitor's product that has been developed and is either currently available for sale or momentarily about to enter market."

Sporkin also argued that even truthful product preannouncements would violate the securities laws, if not the antitrust laws.

The judge had also read the claims that Microsoft developers had unfair access to information about Microsoft's operating systems, giving them an undue advantage over its competitors.

At a subsequent status hearing on November 2, 1994, Sporkin again referred to *Hard Drive*, and told the government he wanted to make sure the book's allegations weren't true.

The DoJ was told to tell interested persons and competitors that they had until December 5 to comment on the consent decree.

On January 10, 1995, over a month late, the law firm of Wilson, Sonsini, Goodrich & Rosati filed a ninety-six-page memorandum on behalf of three unnamed computer companies arguing that the consent decree was inadequate because it would not prevent

Microsoft from monopolizing the rest of the software industry. They claimed that Microsoft had the ability to leverage its installed base in the operating systems market in order to dominate other markets. The firm also attached documents attempting to prove that Microsoft had indeed engaged in vaporware practices.

Ironically, what prompted the allegation was an internal memo from Microsoft itself. A 1987 employee evaluation detailed how Microsoft employee Rob Dickerson took part in the "preannouncing" of a Microsoft product in order to preempt archrival Borland.

To add insult to injury, on February 14, 1995, Sporkin issued an order denying the government's motion to approve the consent decree, stating that "it is too narrow and the parties have been unable and unwilling adequately to address certain anticompetitive practices which Microsoft states it will continue to employ in the future and with respect to which the decree is silent."

The decree had not addressed vaporware. Sporkin was also concerned that it didn't apply to all of Microsoft's operating systems, namely Windows NT.

The judge further noted that "taking into account Microsoft's penchant for narrowly defining the antitrust laws, the Court fears there may be endless debate as to whether a new operating system is covered by the decree."

Microsoft called foul. The company said Sporkin was too biased to make a ruling—*Hard Drive* had contaminated him. Microsoft wanted the case to be remanded to another district court judge. They also took issue with the judge's comments, such as, "Microsoft, a rather new corporation, may not have matured to the position where it understands how it should act with respect to the public interest and the ethics of the marketplace."

On June 16, 1995, a three-judge appeals court ruled unanimously that Sporkin had overstepped his bounds.

With that, the case was assigned to Judge Thomas Penfield Jackson. On August 21, 1995, he entered the consent decree, settling the original antitrust charges and banning Microsoft from linking the licensing of one software product to another.

The feds would continue to investigate Microsoft, and Gates and company from that point on would keep all of their documentation on the premises. Developers said it became part of Microsoft's defensive posturing to accumulate and keep mountains of trash and E-mail around, an avalanche waiting for the next time anyone wanted to know how Microsoft was doing business.

Building 8 looked like an enormous recycling facility. Developers said it wasn't the FTC or the DoJ that Gates should worry about—it was the Redmond fire marshal.

Gates had dodged the first bullets from the federal guns, escaping with maybe a couple of holes in his hat. But the rounds wouldn't stop there. Bill Gates and Judge Thomas Penfield Jackson were heading up the trail toward the O.K. Corral.

13

. . . .

WINDOWS 95—
POWER IN NUMBERS

I think it was a mistake to not just include the browser in Windows 95.

—*Lin Shaw*

The Justice Department's disapproving gaze next turned on Windows, but that didn't really faze the developers. They had enough problems on their own.

From the get-go, as we've seen, the next version of Windows was never thought of as anything more than an upgrade path in the transition to NT, a system that was much more robust, more stable, and a lot more expensive. Code-named "Chicago," this next version would run the old legacy applications, with the advantage that people could also start writing 32-bit applications that would run on it as well as on NT.

In April of 1992, after Windows 3.1 had shipped, two different plans made the rounds. The short-term plan included fixing nasty bugs and fixing the user interface, which was a mess, and which, once again, had never fulfilled Gates's original goal of Windows— *to be like the Mac.* But this was to be nothing more than a new, pretty shell on top of Windows 3.1, with a ship date of June of 1993, hence the name it would briefly carry in-house, Windows 93.

The long-term plan was tied to "Cairo," a far-out skunk-works version of NT with an object-oriented shell and file system. It included redoing the entire operating system and making it 32 bit. The "32 bit" of a 32-bit system referred to how much code the hardware or software could process at once. A 32-bit system *should* run twice as fast as the old 16 bit. But 32 bit didn't always mean faster; it often meant bigger and slower.

Neither plan was particularly well focused, and then six months into it the group realized they didn't have time left to do the short-term plan, the fleeting Windows 93. In order to rationalize the expense of a full-blown beta testing program, they realized they needed a compelling upgrade, and there was hardly time left for that. It also made no sense to turn out yet another version of Windows only a year or so after Windows 3.1, and then another one a year later, thereby upsetting Microsoft's corporate customers.

Brad Silverberg, who was the vice president of the personal operating systems division and overseeing the project, told David Cole to combine both strategies. Cole, the group program manager who had been in charge of the short-term version (a.k.a. Windows 93), would now lead the combined Windows effort (Chicago). Many developers said Cole was the perfect man for the job. He was hands on, very process oriented, and ran an extremely tight organization. His greatest strength, developers said, was his ability to cut through the bullshit and actually ship the product.

One of Cole's first priorities was fixing the new shell.

Satoshi Nakajima, a Microsoft veteran, had worked in the Cairo group since it was first started in late 1988. Cairo, nom de guerre for the future version of NT, had been growing and growing, with architects continually being added to the project, expanding from roughly thirty people to an eventual one hundred. Jim Allchin, the vice president who championed Cairo and later took over NT, began recruiting really "smart" people, generally Ph.D. physicist types who were masters at designing new architectures, but not master hackers, like the so-called dumb developers.

Nakajima was one of the seven members of Cairo's shell team, the group responsible for designing a new "look and feel," or shell interface, for NT. Nakajima, a self-described "dumb" hacker, had been working for several years on the new shell when suddenly all the new "smart" architects came in with ideas for a totally different structure. This meant scrapping the old code that Nakajima had painstakingly written and starting over from scratch. At Microsoft, as we know, this seems to happen every time a new crop of "smart" people shows up.

At the same time, over in Windows-land, the Chicago developers were also talking about building a new shell. The Cairo group saw this as an opportunity. They wanted their shell to become the company standard, one which would stretch across both Chicago, which was slowly evolving into "Windows 95," and Windows NT.

Allchin split the Cairo shell team in half and sent three developers over to Windows, leaving Nakajima behind.

Not long after that, in late 1992, Nakajima's old frustration came back to haunt him again. He was being told that the Cairo group was going to rewrite the shell from scratch. Tired of rewriting code for a product that would never ship, Nakajima wanted to bail.

He took a few days to contemplate a move over to the Windows team. He also went to Allchin and told him he was rewriting too much code that just got trashed. He told him Cairo would never ship.

"Oh, we'll ship," Allchin assured him. "We'll ship Cairo sometime in 1994, so you should stay." Allchin even promised to jump off a bridge if it didn't.

Nakajima directed him to the Golden Gate and joined the Windows 95 team, taking Cairo ideas with him.

Nakajima started writing the new Windows shell in 16-bit code, so it looked and behaved like Cairo. But with the long-term

Windows plan staring them in the face, the Windows 95 developers knew they had to include support for 32-bit applications. This would not be easy. The group had been thinking about 32-bit support, but the question was how much of the system was going to be 32 bit, if any? Was the support simply going to be a thunking layer, a translator that allowed both 16-bit and 32-bit applications to talk to the kernel? And what 32-bit APIs were going to match Windows 95's big-brother operating system, NT?

Some developers in the NT group proposed that the Windows 95 team take the 32-bit NT kernel, and then put the old legacy 16-bit kernel layer on top. After all, the NT team viewed any design, other than their own, as inferior. Naturally, the Windows 95 team proposed the exact opposite. The old 16-bit kernel would sit at the bottom, and the 32-bit layer sat on top. Windows 95 had two kernels so applications could "thunk" between layers, depending on whether it was a 16- or 32-bit application.

The developers on the NT team were not impressed.

But the idea to make Windows 95 32 bit was not on anybody's dance card. What clearly was on the agenda was to make sure that all of the old 16-bit applications, which ran on nearly 90 percent of the world's PCs, would still be able to run on Windows 95. Backward compatibility had been the reason Microsoft was so successful, yet compatibility continued to plague the developers with every version of Windows. As they changed the Windows system, or added new functionality, the threads linking old and new inevitability frayed.

"Applications that Help" helped solve a lot of the compatibility problems. This was a huge database describing the specific behavior of different applications, which was triggered when the application ran or was installed the first time. When a "bad" or incompatible application ran, a little message appeared, telling the user that he or she needed to do something different to make the application run more efficiently. For instance, a message might pop up that suggested purchasing a new software upgrade.

These patches not only helped solve compatibility, they also reduced Microsoft's product support services (PSS) calls, which cost the company upward of $150 million a year. Another tactic Microsoft used to reduce PSS calls was to offer a ninety-day warranty on Windows 95. However, the warranty didn't start until a customer picked up the phone and called Microsoft for help. So if you wanted the warranty to last a long time, you'd better not call PSS.

Lin Shaw had worked on previous versions of Windows, and, eventually, she would become the development manager for Windows 95. Shaw, who was one of only three female developers on the project, would be responsible for the fifty-five developers working on the "core," which included the new shell, user, GDI, and kernel.

One of the biggest challenges for Shaw and long-time comrade David Weise, a nine-year veteran on Windows in charge of GDI, was to fit the operating system into 4MB of RAM. Windows 95 had to run nicely in 8MB but also run in 4MB. Microsoft didn't want to have to tell people that they'd have to go buy more memory to run Windows 95, even if it *was* true.

Brad Silverberg was a devout product guy and hacker at heart who kept the team disciplined by making them work, for a majority of the Windows 95 development, on old 386 and 486 machines. By working on an older machine and seeing how slow the software was, Silverberg argued, the developers were not going to become complacent. Like Soviet architects forced to live on the top floor of their elevatorless buildings, they would realize how their software might run in the real world.

Naturally, developers started complaining. They were the group that made the money for the company. Other Microsoft developers were cruising with 21-inch monitors and two state-of-the-art computers, and they had this crappy, Stalinist development environment.

Nakajima had once enjoyed the luxury of a big monitor and three top-notch 486 machines with 24 megabytes of RAM, but when he moved over from the Cairo group to Windows, he was told he could only have two machines. One of them had to be a 386 box. He too must feel the pain of the end user, he was told, which made for development and debugging with full Soviet speed and efficiency.

But Silverberg was very hands on. When he used the product he could point out countless things that didn't make sense or didn't work. Lin Shaw said the biggest acid test for her team was always, "Would Brad's mom be able to use it?" Silverberg and his internalized "Mom" were the best testers Windows ever had.

The Windows 95 team was much bigger than anything that had ever come before, with eight hundred names in the product's eventual credit list. In addition to the "core" team, networking, and multimedia, Windows 95 also included OLE, the testers, and the documentation people.

With Windows 95, the team had strict rules in place for checking in code and fixing bugs. Hundreds of compatibility issues had to be dealt with. And Shaw, who was simply another developer and cohort on previous versions of Windows, was now a development manager who set up the rules and made sure her team kept the bug count down.

Shaw's group was very close-knit. Her team had worked on the project together for three years, even more for those people who had come from Windows 3.1. They had great esprit de corps. Shaw even held "bug fests," one of which lasted twenty-three days nonstop, including weekends, where the team worked to reduce the bug count down to zero.

In spring of 1994, David Cole called Nakajima.

"In order to make the platform better, we need to develop some real application on top of the Windows system to prove that it's solid and compatible with NT," Cole said. "And you guys should volunteer."

Nakajima and one other developer took on the responsibility for porting the shell from 16 bit to 32 bit. The actual porting, in terms of rewriting the code so that it called the 32-bit APIs correctly and then compiled in a 32-bit way, took two weeks. That was the easy part. The most troubling detail was that the guts of Windows was not stable. The platform was 32 bit, but it wasn't compatible at all. Nakajima tested the shell against 32-bit GDI code, but if the shell made any calls to GDI—crash city. It took more than two months to get the shell to even run on the 32-bit platform, which added yet another delay to the Windows 95 ship date.

But as Windows shell developer Chris Guzak viewed it, "To the degree that the shell was like the initial application that tested the Windows 32 support on Windows 95, that was what drove the success. But if Windows 95 was a failure as a 32-bit platform, no matter how much Windows served as a bridge to future NT versions, we would be massively hosed."

Since November 1994, David Cole had been holding "war meetings" every morning at 9:00 A.M. The war team consisted of Cole, Shaw, the group program manager, the test manager, and the leads for the external groups such as multimedia, networking, and international.

Whenever the team had a new deadline to meet they'd convene again in the conference room at 5:30 P.M. Gates had been receiving regular updates on the team's progress.

In December of 1994, Cole, Shaw, and the rest went back to Gates to discuss the ever-slipping ship date, a result of adding features, changing the shell several times, and incredible hordes of application and hardware compatibility bugs.

Cole leveled with Gates. "We're not going to ship in February."

After Gates calmed down, he huddled with Cole and the team and asked for the facts. In order to come up with the new ship date, they took historical data, and added some padding. They finally came up with a ship date of August 24, 1995, a full seven months away. Like politicians issuing bad news from Washington, they decided Christmas was a good time to announce the new date, so they wouldn't get as much press attention about the latest slip.

"I know I'm going to eat shit, but I'm not going to eat it more than once," Gates told the team.

The revised goal, after Gates's meeting, was to clean up everything for the Windows preview program and have that out by the end of February 1995. Cole knew it would take at least three months for the feedback to come through and for the team to incorporate all of the changes.

Meanwhile, planning for the Windows 95 launch was already well under way.

In January of 1994, Waggener Edstrom began recruiting 100 key editors, 32 analysts, and 150 third-party vendors for the Windows 95 bandwagon. Lining up the national media and the business press was easy. Edstrom had been massaging those relationships for over a decade, sending flowers and cartoons and reminding editors of their spouses' birthdays and wedding anniversaries, earning her "Gates's keeper" reputation. Not only would these people tout Windows 95, they would also be more inclined to show sympathy for Microsoft when competitors started ragging them.

After sixteen months spent seeding the trade press, it was time to think of the end users. For this, Waggener Edstrom leaked exclusive Windows 95 puff stories to all of the important newspapers and publications. The PR firm fed the *New York Times* a story with a marketing twist, the *Wall Street Journal* received a more technical angle, and *People* magazine got an exclusive revealing that NBC's *Friends* sitcom stars Jennifer Aniston and Matthew Perry would be doing a twenty-five-minute video, educating people on the wonders of Windows 95.

Next came the assault on prime time. Commercials were filmed to run before, during, and after the launch. They were targeted for a very specific audience—thirty-five- to fifty-year-olds who made more than $50,000 a year.

All in all, Waggener Edstrom would have twenty months to lather up the press. They could have worked more quickly, of course—but they had to wait for the product.

The PR efforts would play another important role. It had been nearly three years since Windows 3.1 had shipped. During fiscal 1994, Microsoft's revenue growth had slowed to 24 percent, its lowest annual growth rate since going public. Slower growth was reflected in Microsoft's stock price, which appreciated only 50 percent between fiscal 1992 and 1994. The Windows 95 hype would help change all that.

By 1995, Microsoft's installed base of Windows and DOS users had swelled to an estimated 140 million users. As the release date for Windows 95 drew near, Wall Street analysts began to estimate the potential impact that the upgrade might have on the company's growth. Estimating that 20 percent of the installed base upgraded at an average price of $90 per copy, Microsoft could receive a potential $2 billion windfall in a very short period of time. The mere promise of this bonanza broke Microsoft's stock out of its two-year slumber. From June of 1994 to June of 1995, Microsoft shares advanced 75 percent. The company's market value was now $56.7 billion without having shipped a single copy of Windows 95.

Microsoft did sell preview copies, however—$30 a pop to anyone who wanted it—an offer that appealed to 400,000 users. This was Microsoft's way of both making money and at the same time having free beta testers to find the show-stopping bugs, the so-called Severity ones (Sev 1s), that crashed the system. With these unpaid testers, Windows 95 went through more than 75 million hours of testing, the equivalent of a single person sitting down at a computer around the year 6500 B.C. and testing nonstop until 1995. And what the testers found wasn't pretty.

More than 6,000 critical bugs. The team looked for crashing bugs and data-loss bugs. Sometimes they would even fly beta testers' machines back to Redmond, and sometimes they did remote debugging where they debugged testers' machines over the phone.

In early 1995, with Windows scheduled to ship, another crucial and controversial decision was about to be made. It would fuel the ever-growing fire between Silverberg's Windows 95 group and Allchin's NT team.

Like everyone else, Allchin assumed that Windows 95 was merely a short-term project, with Cairo destined to be the ultimate shell, which would run on NT, which would be the successor operating system to Windows 95. Allchin wasn't even threatened by the fact that there was another shell group on another team. His shell, not the Windows 95 shell, would standardize the look and feel of the desktop.

Allchin's Cairo shell developers had written a dissertation-like paper proving that their architecture was superior to the Windows 95 architecture. And in some sense they were right. They had the really good "smart" people architecting everything from scratch, and it was well designed. By contrast, the Windows 95 team started from a 16-bit hacked-up piece of code and then ported the shell out to 32 bits. Accordingly, the Windows code was messy and difficult to maintain, it was not clean and well designed, but it *was* ready to ship.

At this point, Windows 95 had the new shell and NT was still using the old Windows 3.1 interface. At the rate they were going, Windows 95 would be the low-end operating system with the high-end interface. NT would be the high-end operating system with the low-end interface, and Microsoft would look very stupid. The handwriting was on the wall. One of Nakajima's buddies, a fellow "dumb" developer on the Cairo team, started porting the Windows 95 shell over to NT in his spare time.

In the spring of 1995, Gates realized that Microsoft had to make it clear which shell was going to be the ongoing strategy for the company. He called both the Cairo and Windows 95 shell teams into the boardroom. The hour-long meeting was like a multiethnic family reunion in Sarajevo, the two teams staring each other down as Gates struggled to break the news gently. Cairo wasn't dead, he said, it was just being moved to the Outlook group, a personal-information management software project that had yet to ship a product.

All the "smart" people who had been working on the Cairo shell were forced to move, and the "dumb" Cairo people would stay and port the Windows 95 shell to NT, getting it ready to ship with the next version of NT 4.0 the following year.

• • •

As they neared the home stretch, Windows 95 development manager Lin Shaw was not just working until late at night but straight through the weekends. She hired a baby-sitter to care for her daughter, Pauline; at times she dropped her child off in daycare; but most of the time, Shaw brought her little girl to work. Shaw's office already had a TV and VCR, and Pauline knew where the official Microsoft popcorn and pinball machines were. For a while there, Microsoft also had daycare for its employees on weekends, but Pauline didn't like the scene and preferred to hang with her mother.

Still, it wasn't like crunch mode during the Windows 1.0 days when Shaw and her crew slept under their desks and didn't go home for days on end.

With Microsoft's rising stock price, things at the company had actually softened, as had many of the old-time developers' priorities. After a decade or more of death-march projects and 120-hour work weeks, most veteran developers had slowed the pace. Families, friends, and interests outside of Microsoft actually emerged. Sure, developers still worked insane hours during crunch mode, but they also took six-month sabbaticals. Perhaps there were advantages to being a company with, circa 1994, more than 15,000 employees and annual revenues of $4.6 billion.

But with everyone working in full crunch mode and the ship date only three months away, Bill Gates had suddenly discovered the Internet.

On May 26, 1995, Gates issued a memo to his executive staff

turning 180 degrees away from his every previous utterance on the subject. Suddenly, he was stressing the importance of the Net. Suddenly, Field Marshal Gates was encouraging his generals to use it, and unleashing his hordes in a harried race to catch up with his competitors.

"Now I assign the Internet the highest level of importance," Gates said.

> The on-line services business and the Internet have merged. What I mean by this is that every on-line service has to simply be a place on the Internet with extra value added. MSN is not competing with the Internet although we will have to explain to content publishers and users why they should use MSN instead of just setting up their own Web server. We don't have a clear enough answer to this question today. For users who connect to the Internet some way other than paying us for the connection we will have to make MSN very, very inexpensive—perhaps free.

Gates had spent ten hours browsing the Web, and, to his horror, had seen almost no Microsoft file formats. Smelling the scent of blood, he *had* seen a number of his competitors'.

"A new competitor 'born' on the Internet is Netscape. Their browser is dominant, with 70 percent usage share, allowing them to determine which network extensions will catch on," Gates said. "We have to match and beat their offerings including working with MCI, newspapers and others who are considering their products."

Gates made very clear the marching order for this new wave of battle.

> I want every product plan to try and go overboard on Internet features. One element that will be critical is coordinating our various activities. The challenge/opportunity of

the Internet is a key reason behind the recent organization. Paul Maritz will lead the Platform group to define an integrated strategy that makes it clear that Windows machines are the best choice for the Internet. This will protect and grow our Windows asset.

Furthermore, Gates said,

We need to figure out additional features that will allow us to get ahead with Windows customers. We need to move all of our Internet value added from the Plus pack into Windows 95 itself as soon as we possibly can with a major goal to get OEMs shipping our browser preinstalled.

Microsoft had proven time and time again that it would do anything to protect its operating systems business. Now, suddenly, the Internet was the battlefield. But the Windows 95 team was oblivious to the sound of crashing armor and sharpening swords.

As Shaw put it, "The Windows 95 team really had no idea what the Internet was." With only forty-seven days until Windows was released to manufacturing, they were just trying to ship their product, working sixteen-hour days trying to fix all the bugs that had surfaced through the preview program.

Gates had long ago scraped Eller's RIP project—the company's low-bandwidth peer-to-peer Internet effort—in favor of the company's high-bandwidth interactive TV strategy and the company's proprietary on-line service, the Microsoft Network.

Still, after two and a half years of development, MSN lacked content and any clear-cut advantage to show why providers should rent space from MSN rather then set up their own storefronts on the Internet's World Wide Web. Also, the whole time the Windows 95 team kept redesigning the shell, nobody had bothered to tell the

MSN developers. Suddenly they were waking up to the fact that MSN didn't work with Windows 95.

The panicked MSN developers called the Windows 95 shell team.

"Oh yeah," Guzak remembered responding, "we rewrote that."

The MSN team also struggled because so much of Windows 95 on-line technology was still evolving.

Looking back from the vantage of October 1997, Guzak recalled, "A lot of the core functionality we have to support the Internet wasn't there in Windows 95. Winsock [a standard API that provides a TCP/IP interface under Windows] was there, but in a preliminary version, so MSN invented their own protocols. That was one of their major early mistakes. They had their own protocol that was different from TCP/IP."

Still, Microsoft Network was the only on-line card Microsoft was in a position to play. It, not a graphical web browser, was bundled with Windows 95.

Interviewed on July 13, 1997, nine-year Windows veteran Dave Weise described the situation this way: "Even by the time we shipped Windows 95, MSN was in no real shape that anyone would actually be proud of the experience they would get by attaching to it. MSN at that point wasn't even Internet centric. MSN at that point was the AOL model. So no, it wasn't part of some Internet strategy to get MSN in there. Internet strategy comes later."

It was the bundling of MSN that prompted the Department of Justice to once again investigate Microsoft's business practices. Microsoft would once again dodge the bullet, but the issue of bundling applications into the operating system was just getting going, and it would not easily go away, the technical equivalent of Bill Clinton's "bimbo eruptions."

Despite the company's later, well-publicized claims to the contrary, the only Internet technology that made it into the first Windows 95 release was the operating system's ability to establish a dial-up connection to the Internet and to run FTP and Telnet services, archaic, text-based file transfer, and communications front ends.

Consumers who signed up for the new service would search through various topics such as travel and news, only to be met with an annoying message informing them that the service was not yet available. MSN, a proprietary on-line dial-up service, designed to compete with America OnLine and CompuServe, was an instant dinosaur deployed to compete with *Homo robustus,* the World Wide Web.

Nonetheless, Siegelman said in a memo, it was imperative to ship on time with Windows. "We aren't even in the race if we don't launch in August and start getting customers," he wrote.

Still, it would take over a month for the software to hit retailers' shelves, because Microsoft wanted to make sure the channel was stuffed with enough inventory before the launch.

Internally the Windows 95 launch was dubbed "The Sky's the Limit with Windows 95," both because of Windows 95's rainbow-colored flag logo with blue sky in the background, and because of its estimated—including money that PC vendors, retailers, and others would spend—$1 billion marketing campaign. But the real question was how were they going to make this PR splash bigger and better than the last ones, which were already the stuff of legend.

On July 11, Windows 95 went "Golden Master" and was released to manufacturing. The first several hundred copies came back on gold disks to be handed out internally at Microsoft. The disks were souvenirs for the developers who had worked on the project.

On August 24, 1995, riding on Microsoft's unprecedented marketing budget, the perpetually delayed Windows 95 operating system rolled out with a bang in countries around the world. The theme was Midnight Madness.

In an unusual move, Edstrom's minions had New York's Empire State Building lit in the Windows 95 colors. In Britain, copies of the

London *Times* were given away free so people could read a Windows 95 ad supplement. And in southern France, the Windows 95 logo was painted in farmers' fields so that airline passengers overhead wouldn't miss it. Microsoft even paid for rights to the Rolling Stones tune "Start Me Up," used as the Windows 95 theme song.

Hordes of people across the globe lined up outside their local software outlets waiting for the doors to open. Across the nation, computer stores such as CompUSA provided patrons with free pizza and Windows 95 training sessions for the celebration.

As the sun rose in Redmond, Washington, on a luminous August 24, 1995, launch day was already under way in Europe and points east. On its campus, Microsoft set up a pavilion that looked more like a traveling circus and held an all-day celebration hosted by *Tonight Show* host Jay Leno, and, of course, his merry sidekick, Bill Gates.

"I work at the *Tonight Show*, owned by NBC," Leno told the audience, "which now stands for Now Bill (Gates) Compatible." Regarding Gates's technical skills—"I went to his house, and his VCR is still flashing 12:00." And in joking about how Gates had lobbied in Washington in support of Microsoft, Leno said, "Once they heard you could delete files, they had to have it."

Leno provided entertainment for an undisclosed amount, and Gates provided endless platitudes for free. Outside the main circus tent, marquees were set up on Microsoft's sprawling lawn so that hundreds of hardware and software vendors, who paid to participate, could show their wares and their support for Windows 95.

It was all a screaming success, and one of Edstrom's finest moments. During the 20 months preceding the launch, 240 cover stories and 13,000 news stories had run in various publications. Within the 11 days surrounding the launch, Microsoft nabbed 2,000 TV segments. During the two-day launch itself, 100 syndicated radio spots ran. It all looked like news coverage; in fact it was free advertising.

Waggener Edstrom claimed that Microsoft received more media

attention than even the O.J. Simpson trial, which was going on at the same time. Ultimately, 19 million copies of Windows 95 would sell in the four months immediately after its release.

Nonetheless, many people hammered the software for including both a 16-bit and 32-bit kernel, despite the fact that Microsoft had positioned Windows 95 as a true 32-bit operating system. GDI and User were still 16 bit, and much of the memory management calls that 16-bit applications used also called the 16-bit kernel. Some new functionality had been added to support 32-bit applications, but the team had been forced to retain most of the code as 16 bit to keep the legacy applications running. But it was all a major compromise. Even Lin Shaw admitted Windows 95 never reached the performance of Windows 3.1. The team had simply reached the point where they decided that they were close enough and just shipped it.

Microsoft's huge success, as Shaw and other developers freely pointed out, was due to dumb luck. The company had covered the table and some bets paid off.

Corporate adoption and company-wide deployment of Windows 95 turned out to be a major disappointment. In an IDC survey of 400 corporate managers, only 23 percent said they planned to upgrade their PCs to Windows 95 during the first twelve months the product was on the market. Forty-three percent said they wouldn't upgrade during that period and 34 percent didn't know.

Consumers, though, didn't seem to have a problem paying $89 and $109 for the Windows 95 upgrade, but many balked at the extra $50 they had to shell out for Microsoft's Plus Pack, a separate CD that included utilities and other software programs designed to improve the Windows experience. This $50, very un-integrated add-on also contained a web browser. Microsoft had licensed the browser from Spyglass, an application often given away for free on the Internet, and dubbed it Internet Explorer 1.0.

"I think it was a mistake to not just include the browser in Windows 95," said Windows 95 development manager Lin Shaw, when interviewed in September 1997. When asked if there were any discussions about including a browser in Windows 95 she said, "No, not even—even at the time when we shipped we were testing with the Netscape browser, and it wasn't even close."

"IE 1.0 shipped in the Plus Pack," longtime programmer Chris Guzak confirmed, referring again to the $50 add-on carried on a separate CD.

Despite the hype and Microsoft's huge marketing budgets leading up to the Windows 95 launch, by the time fall COMDEX rolled around in November 1995, the Windows 95 operating system was nothing more than a sideshow.

COMDEX excitement, an always fickle commodity, had been diverted to Netscape and its graphical web browser called Navigator. Thousands of hardware and software vendors had scrambled to show how their products were Internet centric, and while most of the computers were running Windows 95 under the hood, what people saw on the screen was not Microsoft's icon, but Netscape's big green N.

Microsoft's efforts to own the Internet had just begun.

14

. . . .

CONTINUAL CHAOS

Are the Mariners going to trade Randy Johnson?
—*Mike Murray*

A t any given time, Microsoft has lagged behind in networking, desktop applications, on-line services, Internet technologies, and Web browsers. And yet the landscape is littered with the bones of Microsoft's competitors: VisiCorp, Lotus, WordPerfect, Novell, GO Corporation. . . . This corporate body count exists because Microsoft has always had one asset that no other company could touch—Windows, which Microsoft could leverage with unrivaled effectiveness.

Their technique had always been to see who was winning, then set its sights to copy, overtake, and crush the competition. So it's no surprise that when Web browsers became mainstream, the Microsoft juggernaut would once again roll into action.

Oddly enough, the browser, this seemingly insignificant application, which Gates had initially dismissed as a "trivial piece of software," had the potential to take down the very empire Chairman Bill and Microsoft had created.

After Windows 95 shipped, once again two plans existed side by side for the *next* version. Initially, the team was working on a short-term version code-named Nashville, and the longer-term plan was dubbed Memphis.

The Nashville team was planning to include some Internet features and to integrate the browser with Windows 95, but the team still had a long list of Windows 95, and even Cairo-oriented, features that they still wanted to put in to enhance the look and feel. The Cairo features included new ways of navigating the computer, but they weren't Internet-like. The team was still in the "hot" phase of development, where everything was being considered, but nothing was clear.

"The Web was just starting to gain momentum," Chris Guzak explained, "and we realized that maybe [the Cairo ideas] weren't the way you should browse your computer. Maybe you should browse your computer like you browse the Web."

"Surprisingly it took a really long time to get that message," said Windows shell and Internet Explorer guru Satoshi Nakajima, "so even though everyone saw Gates's [Internet Tidal Wave] memo saying, 'We're going to the Internet,' it took a really long time for everyone to realize, 'Oh, we have to go to the Internet.'"

"The Internet strategy is typical Microsoft," said fourteen-year Microsoft veteran Steve Wood. "See where everybody's headed then catch up and go past them."

John Ludwig was in charge at the time. David Cole, who had led the Windows 95 project, had since moved over to the consumer group to retrench, but he would soon return to Windows.

In fall 1995, the Windows developers gave Ludwig the list of approximately one hundred new features they wanted to include in the next version.

"The Internet issue had come up, so we put like two Internet features at the bottom [of the list]," Nakajima said.

After looking it over, Ludwig said, "Oh, the Internet features have to be at least twenty percent of the new features, not two percent."

The Windows team went back to the drawing board.

The next meeting went to the next level, with Brad Silverberg, senior vice president in charge of Windows, but he wasn't satisfied with the features either.

"No," Silverberg said. "Eighty percent should be Internet."

Frustrated, the Windows developers went back to the drawing board again.

The next meeting with Silverberg was no different, only this time he said, as Nakajima put it, "Every feature has to be Internet."

"There was kind of a delay of the message from Gates to the high-level execs to us," Nakajima said.

On December 8, 1995, less than two weeks after Internet Explorer 2.0 shipped, Gates announced his new Internet strategy. In short, it was a regurgitation of his May "Tidal Wave" memo, only sanitized for the public.

"We are hard core about the Internet," Gates said. "Today the Internet is the primary driver of the new work we're doing across our entire product line." Yet so pervasive was this new technology that, as Gates would later add, "We're not forming an Internet division. That would be like having an electricity division or a software division."

Gates announced that Microsoft, in an atypical move, had acquired the rights to license Java, the widely adopted, lightweight scripting language for the Internet from archrival Sun Microsystems.

But for all his new Internet fervor, Gates was still an MSN kind of guy. At this time he renamed Microsoft's yet-to-be-released set of software tools for developing content on the Microsoft Network—"Blackbird" became "Internet Studio."

Gates said that Internet Studio would now support not only MSN, but the entire Internet. Within two months, the project was canceled.

On February 20, 1996, Gates ate his words about that "electricity division" he had disdained only two months before. Microsoft would now have an Internet platform and tools group to bring the Windows strategy in line with the Internet.

Silverberg was appointed as its senior vice president.

Microsoft's long-envisioned, but still unrealized, Grand Convergence of all operating systems was finally beginning to unfold. The only grand operating system to be left standing, as indicated by the reorganization, would be NT—not Windows. Once again, the old core asset, worth billions of dollars annually to Microsoft, was to be maintained merely as a transitional pathway.

What was it with these guys?

Jim Allchin, who had been leading Cairo and NT, would now take on responsibilities for the entire Windows platform. His official title was Senior Vice President, Desktop and Business Systems division. He and Silverberg both would report to Paul Maritz, who was appointed group vice president, platforms.

When Windows 95 shipped in August 1995, NT version 3.51 was on the market, but it lacked the new Windows 95 user interface, because Allchin had resisted taking Silverberg's Windows 95 shell. So one of the first steps toward merging the operating systems now meant giving NT a face-lift.

As NT old-timer Steve Wood put it, "If we want to have Windows 95 go away and never come back, we have to put the Windows 95 features into NT."

"It made us look stupid as a company. And it makes NT look stupid," Wood continued, "cause here we are the high-end system with the low-end interface. That's Bill's fault for not setting a strategic direction that made sense and enforcing it, forcing the two groups to come up with a solution that made sense and shared code."

The Windows 95 developers agreed.

"When Windows 95 was out and NT 3.51 was the platform, things were massively screwed up," said Chris Guzak, who had worked on the Windows 95 shell. "The interfaces were different and the programming models were far enough apart that they caused a lot of pain for [software developers]."

"It's been like that ever since I've been here," Wood added. "The direction never comes from on top. Bill would never take Brad Silverberg and Paul Maritz in the same room and say, 'I don't give a shit about your two problems or your two groups, I want the same API set on both systems, and I want them compatible, and I want tests that prove it. It's your problem. I don't care what you have to do. You can't ship until that's true.' "

After Gates's February 20, 1996, announcement, with the reorganization imminent, many programmers could see that once again Windows was considered a short-term product, which meant that Windows people would not be doing innovative work.

Developers could move over into Allchin's group, where the core of the next version of Windows would live, or they could stay with Silverberg's clan, where the Internet Explorer shell (Nashville) was being built. It wasn't a hard decision. Most of the people, including Shaw and Nakajima, went to work on Internet Explorer.

Roughly forty people from the Windows 95 team migrated into Allchin's group, where they focused on the long-term Windows 95 upgrade, dubbed "Memphis," but soon to be known as Windows 98.

"Windows 98 is just to support new hardware—the new device-driver model so that the same device driver can work on Windows 98 and NT," said Lin Shaw. "That's what Windows 98 is, a lot of new hardware support and a new shell. Windows 98 is just trying to make it faster. In my opinion it's like a .1 release of Windows 95."

Simply to give Microsoft consumers a reason to upgrade, Microsoft eventually would put the new Internet Explorer 4.0 shell on top. By putting IE in Windows, Microsoft also could rationalize the exorbitant expense of building the new shell, which as Internet Explorer, they were giving away free.

"Ultimately," Guzak said, "investing almost a whole division in an unprofitable development effort—IE—is going to have to end at some point."

Microsoft refused to put the upgraded Windows 95 on the retail shelves. Short of buying a new computer, the only way to get the latest version would be to buy Windows 98, or spend hours downloading updates and patches from Microsoft's Web site.

"Microsoft doesn't want to have to support five versions of Windows. Microsoft still has different versions of Windows 95, but the OEM has to answer the call," said Wood. "Microsoft only has to support one copy of Windows. So Windows 98 will sell to all those people out there who have refused to take all the time to download all the random patches to Windows 95."

Analysts predicted that, even with such a slender rationale for its existence, Windows 98 would generate revenues of $3 billion over two years.

In February 1996, while the small Memphis team worked on the long-term Windows upgrade, a.k.a. Windows 98, the Internet Explorer 3.0 group went on a frenzied hiring spree. It appeared they had to.

At that time, according to Zona Research in Redwood City, California, Internet Explorer had only 3 percent of the market, compared with Netscape Navigator's 74 percent. But what really goaded the Microsoft developers were comments by Marc Andreessen, Netscape's senior vice president of technology.

"I think ultimately Netscape painted a big target on themselves with Marc Andreessen's inflammatory comments about Windows 95 being a device-driver layer and not a fully debugged one at that," said IE developer Chris Guzak. "I remember talking with people in the halls and seeing guys like John Ludwig so pissed, and having those guys read back this stuff to me, John and Brad, it just pissed those guys off so much. I think as much as anything that motivated a lot of the early Internet work.

"It was like 'those assholes,'" Guzak added. "I'm going to make their stock options worth nothing. We were already competing with them anyway because we were building Explorer, but that just added fuel to the fire. Netscape was kicking our butt at that point."

Guzak said he remembered looking at Netscape Navigator's new frames features, which made the screen far more appealing, trying to figure out how to include frames like that in Explorer. "Frames probably happened a month earlier cause these [Microsoft] guys were so pissed," he said. "They stayed in their office and finished coding."

In February 1996, when the new Internet group was set up, two versions of Internet Explorer were being developed simultaneously. Originally the IE 4.0 team was going to be completely independent from the IE 3.0 group. But Nakajima started writing some code to prove that the IE 4.0 team could take over the user-interface component of IE 3.0. The Spyglass software Microsoft had licensed was a big integrated chunk of code that made up the entire browser. This included the hypertext markup language rendering code, which would draw the screen; the download code, which enabled users to retrieve files from the Web; the navigation code, which allowed users to go to Web sites; and the frame shell, or user interface, which gave the browser its look and feel.

Nakajima started hacking to split the code into two distinct pieces.

In order to integrate the browser with the operating system, Microsoft had to first separate the HTML rendering engine from the browser's user interface. That way, Microsoft could replace the Windows user interface with the browser's, and the rendering engine would simply become part of the operating system.

"We kind of knew that we were going to integrate the browser into the shell," said Nakajima, "but IE 3.0 was not the right time frame."

IE 4.0 would take over a year to develop, and it would be the version of Internet Explorer that would allow the browser to take over the desktop, allowing Windows and the browser at long last to be truly integrated.

When Microsoft shipped IE 4.0 on October 1, 1997, the DoJ quickly took notice. At issue was the question of whether

Microsoft was illegally leveraging Windows to get a strong hold in the browser market.

In the February 1996 reorg, according to various developers, Paul Maritz had decided that there would be only one shell team for the entire company, and it would be Guzak's team sitting in Silverberg's organization. The idea was to have one single-user interface—a step toward the Grand Convergence.

Allchin was irate. He had already been forced to take the Windows 95 shell and put it into NT 4.0, which would ship in the summer of 1996. Now he would have to take the Internet Explorer 4.0 shell for NT 5.0, which wouldn't ship at least until late 1998. The NT group was tired of taking other groups' code, code over which they had no control.

In April 1997, the fighting between the NT group and the IE 4.0 shell group had become so intense that Paul Maritz had to step in. For a week, Maritz met with the IE team for one hour every day to figure out how to make the working relationship with the NT team work.

The NT group said they weren't getting enough of a commitment from the IE team to deliver a shell. The IE developers argued that there was no way they could meet the NT team's demands without slipping IE 4.0. The IE team asked Maritz what they should do.

Maritz layed down the law. Shipping IE 4.0 on time was first priority, the second priority was servicing the Memphis team (Windows 98), and the last item on the agenda was delivering a version of Internet Explorer 4.0 to Windows NT 5.0.

"NT 5.0 was still about a year away," said Guzak. "Certainly we pimped them at the price of getting IE 4.0 out on time."

When the IE code crashed, the NT developers called for help. "Can you come look at this?"

"We've got our own problems," was the response. "It doesn't crash on Windows 95, so we don't care."

Faced with few options, the NT developers decided that when

they received a piece of IE code that was relatively stable, the NT team would just use it. That would be why, on September 23, 1997, when the first NT 5.0 beta shipped, it was running a three-month-old version of Internet Explorer—marginal at best.

Steve Wood concluded by saying he'd run the NT 5.0 beta on his desktop at work, but no way was he going to install it on his home machine.

"I run it on my desktop and half the time I go to an IE window and I try to type text in the little Web address . . . it access violates as soon as I type," said Wood. "I've got to relaunch it."

The IE team wasn't interested in fixing three-month-old bugs for NT and, furthermore, the NT team shouldn't have used old IE code in the first place.

"That was a bad decision," said Guzak. "They could have guessed that IE would have slipped its ship date another month or two, and NT would have still made their original beta date, and it would have been a good decision."

"What I blame is the fact that upper management allowed the situation to get to that point in the first place," said Wood.

By May 1997, Gates was touting Windows NT as the future of the company. The PR spin was evident when Gates graced the cover of *Fortune* magazine's May 26 issue.

"Gates' Greatest Power Grab (It's Working)," the cover read.

"Forget the Internet. Forget MSNBC. Windows NT, Bill Gates' new software for corporate networks is the real future of Microsoft," the headlines declared.

Suddenly, NT had become Gates's long-awaited strategic vision. "It's fair to say Microsoft has bet its future on Windows NT version 5.0," Gates said at an industry conference in September.

At the Seybold computer conference in October, Gates told an audience, "In '98, once we ship NT 5.0, the message to business users will be very clear, that we want to help you move to Windows NT."

Microsoft hoped the transition would be simple.

"NT 5.0 is supposed to be the real end-user thing," said Guzak. "It has to subsume the Windows 95 code base, and then there is no need for Windows."

However, he added in a cautionary note, "If NT 5.0 can't fulfill something that I'll install on my mom's machine, we're in a bad way."

•   •   •

Meanwhile, the IE 4.0 team was in a race with Netscape.

The fastest way to deliver software was via the Net. On October 1, 1997, the next version of Internet Explorer went up on Microsoft's home page for people to access.

Microsoft said that within the first forty-eight hours, more than one million copies of IE 4.0 were downloaded. But while Internet delivery was fast, it was also less stable and prone to more bugs.

"Fortunately if you find a bug, then you can post that on the Web and follow up," said Guzak. "We fixed a bug twenty-three hours before the first person downloaded it off the Web . . . and we introduced a new bug because of that fix. Now that's scary."

Which was why IE 4.0 went out the door late.

Still, the software was praised by many in the press.

"Microsoft's new Internet Explorer browser and its companion Outlook Express mail package are decisively superior to the latest version of Netscape's Navigator browser and Messenger E-mail software," said *Wall Street Journal*'s Walt Mossberg. "That's bad news for those who think the company has too much power."

Mossberg went as far as to say that not only did he recommend the products, they were among the best programs Microsoft had ever published.

This was welcome news for the IE 4.0 team, especially knowing that their boss, senior vice president Brad Silverberg, listened carefully to Mossberg.

"Walt keeps us in line with things like simplicity, keeping Windows easy to use," said Guzak. "Because ultimately we traded some of that for business relationships and leverage with our platform in IE 4.0. We put all these logos of all these companies on millions of people's desktops. Hopefully, that information will be useful, but mostly it was, 'We want these people to be invested in our platform and have them care about it, publish for it, etc.' And the best way to do that was to give them a little space on the desktop."

Which was a practice for which Mossberg roundly criticized Microsoft.

When Microsoft launched IE 4.0, the team delivered a present to Netscape's headquarters in Mountain View, California. At 1:35 in the morning, members of the IE team left a sixteen-foot giant E on their rival's front lawn. Attached was a card that said, "GOOD people shouldn't have to feel so BAD! Best Wishes!—the IE team."

The future was looking bright for Microsoft. The company reported revenues of $3.13 billion for the fiscal first quarter ending September 30, a 36 percent increase over the $2.30 billion reported in the same quarter of 1996.

And then the Justice Department came back with a vengeance.

On October 20, 1997, Attorney General Janet Reno announced that the DoJ had filed a complaint in federal court, asking that Microsoft be stopped from tying its Internet Explorer to Windows 95. The government said that by bundling the products together, Microsoft was in violation of its 1995 consent decree, the agreement that prohibited Microsoft from imposing anticompetitive licensing terms on PC makers. Joel Klein, head of the Justice Department's antitrust division, called the practice "an abuse of monopoly power." Not surprisingly, he added, "And we will seek to put an end to it."

In the Justice Department's petition filed with the court, the DoJ wrote:

"The threat that competing browsers present to Microsoft's

monopoly has two primary aspects: first, the degree to which browsers may become accepted as an interface; and second, the extent to which they can serve as a platform to which applications can be written that are independent of the underlying operating system."

In other words, according to the government, it is okay for a browser to compete with an OS, yet it is not okay for an OS to incorporate browser functionality to try to compete with a browser.

In its complaint, the government demanded that:

- Microsoft stop requiring PC makers to take Internet Explorer as a condition of receiving Windows 95,
- notify PC users with Windows 95 that they are not required to use IE and provide them with instructions to remove the Explorer icon if they choose,
- Strike down broad portions of nondisclosure agreements it requires its customers to sign,
- Pay a $1-million-a-day fine until actions are taken.

Several states' attorneys general, including those from California, New York, Texas, Minnesota, Florida, Oregon, Illinois, Massachusetts, and Connecticut joined the anti-Microsoft crusade by launching their own probes. The states were seeking a "tobaccolike" multistate antitrust settlement. Adding to Gates's woes, this was coupled with government investigations under way in Europe and Asia.

"Microsoft is going to find that it is looking at a shotgun with multiple barrels," said Gary Reback, a lawyer with the firm of Wilson, Sonsini, Goodrich & Rosati in Palo Alto, California, which represents a slew of Microsoft's competitors.

Microsoft's case wasn't helped any when an executive from Compaq Computer Corp., one of Microsoft's largest customers, said in a deposition that Compaq had originally planned to offer Netscape's browser with Windows.

"When they [Microsoft] found out about it, they sent a letter to us telling us that, you know, they would terminate our agreement [Compaq's Windows license] for doing so," said Stephen Decker, director of software procurement for Compaq. The company retreated.

Microsoft responded by saying that the browser was simply a new feature of Windows that it had been planning to include since 1993.

In his November 8 affidavit, Brad Chase, vice president of developer relations and Internet marketing, stated, "Microsoft has always viewed the Internet technologies referred to as IE, including Web-browsing functionality, as an integral part of Windows 95. Going back to 1993 and 1994, our work on Internet technologies has always been directed toward incorporating them into our operating systems."

Microsoft project leader Benjamin Slivka agreed in his December 2 affidavit. "The DoJ states that 'Internet Explorer was not designed or "developed" to be an integrated product with Windows 95' [DoJ reply brief 12]. This is also untrue. From the very outset, my development team—which was part of the overall Chicago development team—was building Internet Explorer as an integrated feature of Windows 95."

On November 10, 1997, Microsoft filed its response to the Justice Department's October 20 petition, arguing that Internet Explorer is, in fact, an integrated part of Windows 95, and that Microsoft is therefore allowed to require OEMs to install all of Windows 95, including its Internet Explorer elements.

"As a result of the DoJ's unwillingness or inability to understand the facts surrounding Microsoft's inclusion of Internet-related technologies in Windows 95, the DoJ's papers are replete with inaccurate factual assertions. For instance, the DoJ asserts that what it defines as a 'browser' is able to access information on the hard-disk drive of a computer 'without interacting with the underlying operating system on the PC' [DoJ memo 31]. That statement is absurd and reflects a profound confusion about the nature of the relationship between Internet Explorer and other elements of Windows 95."

Microsoft executives took turns pounding their chests to defend the company and its operating system monopoly. On October 22, 1997, Steve Ballmer even went so far as to say, with uncharacteristic singularity, "To heck with Janet Reno."

"It's our product and we get to define what's in it," said William Neukom, Microsoft's senior vice president for law and corporate affairs. Sounding every bit as thermonuclear as his name, he added, "If PC makers choose to license it, they are not entitled to pick and choose from among the functions."

At Microsoft's shareholder meeting in November 1997, Captain Gates circled his wagons and began firing in all directions.

"Our decision to put browser technology into the operating system actually predates the founding of Netscape," Gates said. "It was not a decision that was made based on some view of competitive dynamics. It was simply a natural progression of putting integrated features into our operating system."

In his talk to shareholders, Gates went on to refer to the DoJ's investigation as a "witch hunt."

The first major lawsuit to hit Microsoft, the one where Apple claimed to have invented the trash can, had hit like a bombshell. The developers wondered what they should do. The lawyers basically said, "Talk to no one and 'press on.' We'll deal with this." By the time the FTC action rolled around where they were looking for collusion with IBM at a time when the two could not sit in the same room together, it became clear that legal actions were like forest fires, random and raging; they burn out, and win or lose, they cost many years and dollars. The developers were getting the message: you build a tall steeple, it attracts lightning. Hire a few more lawyers, nail on a few more lightning rods, and keep on trucking.

IE developer Satoshi Nakajima loved working on a product that was getting so much attention. "Like the antitrust thing about the shell and the browser being integrated," he said. "It was like, 'Yeah, I did that!' so that feeling is almost addictive. You feel like 'Yes! Yes! Yes!' "

Another Microsoft employee said, "It's a nonevent here. There's an attitude that the Justice Department probably doesn't know how to read its own consent decree, so you should just keep doing what you're doing."

It seemed a decade of federal investigations has made the Softies somewhat blasé. As another employee put it, "Oh, there's another legal action today. Okay. Pass the salt."

Added Microsoft spokesman Mike Murray, "The big deal out here right now is, 'Are the Mariners going to trade Randy Johnson?' "

On December 11, U.S. District Court Judge Thomas Penfield Jackson issued a preliminary injunction. He ruled that Microsoft must stop, at least temporarily, forcing computer makers to install its Internet browser program as a condition for licensing Windows. He did, however, set aside the $1 million a day in penalties. Similarly, he rescinded the order that Microsoft cancel its nondisclosure agreements in its licensing contracts with computer vendors.

Judge Penfield Jackson didn't rule on the contempt charges, but rather appointed Harvard Law School professor Lawrence Lessig as a "special master" to advise the court, and to file by May 31 a full report on the issues raised, as well as a proposed resolution in the contempt charge.

"We see this as a balanced decision," said a Microsoft spokesman. "We are gratified with a number of provisions in the ruling."

On December 15, to comply with the judge's orders, Microsoft responded by offering two new versions of the Windows 95 operat-

222 • BARBARIANS LED BY BILL GATES

ing system to computer makers: one that was antiquated and one that simply didn't work.

"The court requires us to provide Windows 95 without the Internet Explorer files," said Brad Chase, Microsoft's vice president of Internet marketing. "Unfortunately when you take out those files, you are left with a version of Windows 95 that doesn't boot."

In court papers filed on December 15, Microsoft gathered up its full, righteous indignation to declare, "By forcing Microsoft to license such a dysfunctional product to computer manufacturers under the trade name 'Windows,' the district court's order will irreparably injure Microsoft's reputation.

"In addition, the court's preliminary injunction applies to 'any successor version' of Windows 95, i.e., to Windows 98. The district court's inclusion of Windows 98—an extremely complex product that has been under development at Microsoft for more than two years—in its preliminary injunction has given rise to rampant speculation that Windows 98 may have to be redesigned and that the release of Windows 98 will be delayed as a result."

God forbid a Windows delay!

Three days earlier, Greg Shaw, a spokesman for Microsoft, had been quoted in the *San Jose Mercury News* as saying the ruling would *not* affect Microsoft's plans or the ship date.

Microsoft went on to say that significant segments of the United States economy might be affected by doubt surrounding the release of Windows 98. Microsoft claimed this was a reasonable assertion, as demonstrated by the precipitous decline in the Dow Jones Industrial Average (15 points in a matter of minutes) when rumors circulated in late June 1995 that Microsoft had delayed the release of Windows 95.

Microsoft also announced it was appealing Judge Jackson's preliminary injunction, which required the company to unbundle Windows and Internet Explorer, saying that it was in "error" for imposing it in the first place. Microsoft also asked the court of appeals to expedite their consideration of Microsoft's appeal.

By December 18, things turned sour for the Soft.

Irritated by Gates's coy response to the "unbundling" order, the Justice Department accused Microsoft of making a mockery of Federal Judge Penfield Jackson's decision.

The DoJ's court papers stated, "Microsoft's naked attempt to defeat the purpose of the court's order and to further its litigation strategy is an affront to the court's authority; the court accordingly should hold Microsoft in civil contempt and act swiftly to bring it into compliance."

The Justice Department also renewed its request that the court fine Microsoft $1 million a day for contempt and, in an unusual move, asked the judge to give the government new authority to review any new operating systems or browsers made by Microsoft at least thirty days before release.

Suddenly, it seemed everyone wanted a piece of the Microsoft action. Even former senate majority leader Bob Dole, as part of a lobbying effort, sent letters and called companies to get their support in expanding the campaign against the evil Gates Gang.

In a letter to one company, Dole wrote, "In the coming months, we will need to educate the public, the administration, and Congress about the dangers of a laissez-faire attitude toward Microsoft. I am personally convinced that if nothing is done now, it will become increasingly difficult to have fair competition in the years ahead. That is why we will need companies like yours to help finance and support our efforts."

Jody Powell, former press secretary to President Carter, and now an influential Washington lobbyist, also lined up to give Microsoft a few whacks. At the same time, the European Commission, which oversees legal disputes for member countries, was conducting its own probe into Microsoft's practices in the European Union, one of the company's most valuable markets. European revenues represented 22 percent, or a little more than $2.5 billion of Microsoft's total sales for fiscal 1997.

For its part, the Progress and Freedom Foundation, a conservative think tank tightly associated with House Speaker Newt Gingrich, set up a forum on Microsoft and antitrust laws.

On December 19, Judge Penfield Jackson, in an experiment reminiscent of Richard Feynman's ice-water dunk of the *Challenger*'s O-ring, easily removed the Internet browser icon from the Windows 95 desktop. It took his technician less than ninety seconds and six key strokes to rebut Microsoft's argument. But Microsoft didn't just take their lumps and go home to watch *It's a Wonderful Life.* Petitioning again, they said Judge Penfield Jackson's decision to appoint a "special master" was not appropriate and that the company would challenge it. On December 23 Microsoft did just that and filed a motion to remove Lawrence Lessig from the case.

The day before Christmas, Microsoft stock fell $4.375 to $118.94 a share, a seven-month low, a decline of 21 percent from its summer highs of slightly over $150. Over 11 million shares traded on the NASDAQ. Analysts said it was a direct result of the Justice Department's investigation.

Since Microsoft had peaked in the summer of 1997, the value of Gates's 20.5 percent stake in the company had dropped by $8 billion—down to a mere $32 billion.

Adding injury to insult, analysts who had long supported Microsoft said that the company's harsh language in court filings and public statements was turning the case into a public-relations nightmare.

In trying to get rid of Lessig, Microsoft argued the law, but they also argued bias.

"Under court rules, unless the parties consent, special masters can only be appointed for specific and limited purposes, which are not applicable in this case," William Neukom, Microsoft's legal expert opined. "These rules exist to protect the parties' constitutional right to have their federal cases heard by a federal judge."

Furthermore, he cited an E-mail message Lessig had sent six months before.

Lessig, who holds a master's degree in philosophy from Cambridge as well as a law degree from Yale, is an avid computer hobbyist. He is also widely considered to be one of the world's leading thinkers on the intersection of the law and the Internet.

On July 29, 1997, he had sent an E-mail to Netscape attorney Peter Harter, complaining about problems he'd encountered with Internet Explorer after he loaded the program onto his Macintosh.

"Okay, this is making me really angry, and Charlie Nesson," Lessig said, referring to another professor at Harvard Law School, "thinks we should file a lawsuit."

Ironically, Lessig had only installed the Microsoft software because he wanted to enter a contest the company was sponsoring, hoping to win a free Mac laptop. But doing this, he said, "screwed up" his Netscape bookmarks. He summed up the whole experience by saying he had "sold my soul and nothing happened."

Microsoft was furious that, instead of calling up Microsoft tech support, Lessig had complained to their chief rival. Microsoft, of course, took their wounded pride to the Net, posting the E-mail on its Web site, and including Lessig's phone number and address at work, along with the Netscape contacts.

Nuke 'em, indeed.

"This kind of smoking-gun proof of bias underscores the serious flaws in the court's actions," said a Microsoft spokesman.

Microsoft demanded that Lessig recuse himself, saying, "Microsoft regards the sentiments expressed by you and your acquaintances at Netscape as exhibiting clear bias against Microsoft, disqualifying you from any further participation in this case."

Lessig refused.

Unimpressed, the Justice Department said Microsoft's claims were "unfounded and overblown."

Then on January 8, 1998, just five days before Microsoft's contempt hearing was scheduled, the company did an about-face.

Booming Steve Ballmer, Gates's number two, said the company

had received an outpouring of mail from customers, much of it saying that the company was too arrogant.

He cited one that read, "I don't want your products to be like Philip Morris; I don't want to have to go outside to use them."

"People view us as more powerful than we view ourselves," Ballmer announced. "So there's more fear and maybe more of a need for us to be fair, not just even in our dealings, but overly sensitive."

He went on to say he regretted the "unfortunate statement" he had made when he said "to heck with Janet Reno." Obviously, he was getting more sensitive already.

Robert Herbold, Microsoft's chief operating officer and executive vice president, summed it up with, "We need to do a better job of toning down the rhetoric."

Microsoft spokesman Mike Murray took the unusual step of actually *apologizing*: "Over the past two months, some people have perceived Microsoft as being disrespectful to the court and the Department of Justice, and we are very sorry to have created that impression."

Then they went right back into the ring and started throwing punches.

On January 13, 1998, Microsoft went to the U.S. district court in Washington, D.C., to fight the Justice Department's charge that Microsoft had shown contempt for Jackson's court order.

DoJ attorney Phillip Malone said that instead of simply using the "add/remove" option in Windows 95, which deletes the Internet Explorer icon but which leaves critical underlying files, "Microsoft took an extreme and illogical approach" in complying with the court by offering a useless version of Windows 95.

Microsoft's attorneys argued that the company was in full compliance. They said that the company had carefully reviewed government documents before deciding how to comply with the judge's order.

"The government got what it wanted, knowing full well what the consequences would be," said Microsoft attorney Richard J. Urowsky.

"What the government requested is not the same as what I ordered," Jackson fired back.

"I beg to differ with you," Urowsky said. He said that Microsoft had done exactly what the Justice Department requested—Microsoft unbundled IE from Windows—which resulted in a nonfunctional operating system.

DoJ attorney Malone said the judge's order was broad and left Microsoft with room for interpretation.

Meanwhile, the Fair Trade Commission announced its own probe and showed up in Tokyo and searched Microsoft's Japanese subsidiary. The commission was not only looking into whether Microsoft was in violation of the antimonopoly law by marketing Windows and Internet Explorer together, but was also considering the legality of the bundling tactics for its word processor and spreadsheet package.

On January 14, 1998, Microsoft attorneys showed up in court with Microsoft's vice president of consumer platform business, David Cole.

Cole tried to convince Judge Penfield Jackson that Microsoft could not meet the court's order simply by using Windows 95's add/remove function.

"Even though we ran the add/remove utility, Internet Explorer is still there," Cole said. "The code is still there."

The judge then asked about loading rival Netscape's browser on Windows 95. "Would that in any way affect the system?" Jackson asked.

"Of any of the features I described, no," Cole said.

By the end of Cole's testimony, the judge seemed exasperated.

In summarizing Microsoft's position, Judge Jackson said, "It seemed absolutely clear to you that I entered an order that required that you distribute a product *that would not work?* Is that what you're telling me?"

"In plain English, yes," Cole replied. "We followed that order—it wasn't my place to consider the consequences of that."

Later that day, spitting nails, the judge threw out Microsoft's motion to have Special Master Lessig removed from the case. Jackson said that the issues Microsoft cited for having Lessig removed were "trivial and altogether nonprobative. They are, therefore, defamatory, and the court finds they were not made in good faith."

Microsoft spokesman Greg Shaw said, "We're naturally disappointed with the decision. We felt that the evidence spoke for itself. We'll naturally work with Professor Lessig as we have up to this point."

The *New York Times* characterized the DoJ's opinion of the Cole episode by saying that his testimony "illustrates Microsoft's hubris, and showed that the software giant was deliberately thumbing its nose at the government and the federal bench."

Small wonder, then, as Cole's testimony also made clear, that Microsoft's response to the order had been personally crafted by Microsoft Chairman William H. Gates III.

· ·

EPILOGUE

On January 3, 1998, the *New York Times* op-ed page carried a parody of John Steinbeck's novel called "Of Mice and Men, Release 2.0."

In it, the modern-day George says to the modern-day Lennie, "And if that ain't bad enough, now Microsoft wants to make it a rule that every new baby borned from here on out comes bundled from the stork with its own Web browser."

"Not the little babies, too, George!"

"At least that seems to be the gist of it. Janet Reno's suin' Bill Gates a million bucks a day for sayin' so, and that means he'll be out of dough in approximately never, so don't look for no sudden improvements. It's all like Monopoly money to him anyhow."

One day after that, the *Times* carried a special business section, which was, essentially, a full-page apotheosis of Microsoft. On the left, in two full-length columns, ran a chart listing the company's acquisitions, partnerships, alliances, and joint ventures since 1995. Ranging from such substantial partners as NBC, Dreamworks, and even former rival Apple, to investments in smaller companies like Uunet and E-Stamp, the chart lists a total forty-seven links within the world of high technology, communications, and entertainment.

Images of Frank Norris's *The Octopus* came to mind, but the *Times*'s business reporters did not make the allusion.

"Where Microsoft Wants to Go Today" is the headline of the accompanying article. It speaks of Microsoft's fantastic year, its many expansive investments, its $9 billion in cash, and its total absence of debt.

"I've competed against Microsoft for years," Novell chairman Eric Schmidt is quoted as saying. "But I never quite appreciated how big Microsoft has become, not just as a company, but as a brand and as part of the national consciousness. It's the products, the Microsoft marketing juggernaut, Bill Gates's wealth, all those magazine cover stories. It's everything."

"All of which," the *Times* says elsewhere in the piece, "makes competing against Microsoft an uphill battle."

•   •   •

That same week, on the other side of the continent, Netscape chief executive James Barksdale had a painful task to perform. From the company's Mountain View, California, headquarters he announced that Netscape would report losses for both the fourth quarter and for the year. Netscape's shares immediately lost more than a fifth of their value. It was the first time Netscape reported a loss from operations since it went public in August 1995.

"While our products are doing extremely well in the marketplace," said Mike Homer, Netscape's vice president of sales and marketing, "and we're fighting the market-share battle effectively, the revenue is what is being diminished based on price pressure from Microsoft's free browser."

Netscape's stock had been heading south, and on January 9, 1998, would plummet to just under $18—down from $48 in July—a far cry from its all-time high of $85.50 in pre-Windows December 1995.

Netscape was being forced to cut up to 15 percent of its work force, resulting in the layoff of at least four hundred people. In order to compete with Microsoft, Netscape would have to give away its Navigator browser, which represented 13 percent of its revenues in the fourth quarter. Browser sales had fallen to $17 million in the quarter from $52 million the year before. The market valuation was down to $1.68 billion from $5.37 billion.

Who knows what thoughts passed through the head of Jim Barksdale or Jim Clark as they watched their hard-won empire crumble. One thinks of Roman plutocrats in the last days, watching nervously the council fires of Vandals or Visigoths, those hungry barbarians encircling their villas or camped outside their city gates, waiting with sharpened sticks to pillage, and plunder, and rape.

Certainly the Netscape experience was different in that their decline was so precipitous, the flip side of their rocketlike ascendance.

Perhaps, then, the greater commonality between modern and ancient is the bond between the encircled men of Netscape and that other band of warriors, the Trojan armies, who, after a long siege, were the first to learn the dangers of a freebie—in their case, a very large wooden horse.

Certainly, as we consider how Netscape was undone by that free Web browser, we must remember the immortal lesson gained by the sons of Priam three thousand years ago in the ancient city of Troy—beware of geeks bearing gifts.

. . . .

NOTES

vii   *"Actually, my . . . the skill?"*: Bill Gates interview with *Playboy* magazine, July 1, 1994.

Prologue

4   *"An Internet . . . of software."*: Gates speech to analysts, December, 1995.

4   *83 percent versus 8 percent.*: Zona Research, September 29, 1997.

1. The Road Behind

5   *"Formats and Protocols for Consumer Information."*: Nathan Myhrvold interoffice memo, August 30, 1992.

9   *"I believe . . . of them."*: Ibid.

10   *"They weren't . . . around you."*: David Marquardt, interview with *Business Week*, July 15, 1996.

10   *"His view . . . interesting business?"*: Ibid.

11   *The idea . . . go on-line.*: "Issues for RIP," Nathan Myhrvold
      internal memo, December 27, 1992.

2. The Making of the Microsoft Marketing Machine

23   *Remala was . . . Apple's Macintosh.*: Neil Konzen E-mail, De-
      cember 17, 1997. He wrote: "I remember only Dan McCabe with
      the docs [Apple Computer's Macintosh documentation] in his
      hands."
24   *Wood knew . . . the place.*: Steve Wood interview, August 22,
      1995.
25   *"We don't . . . strategic standpoint."*: Ibid.
25   *"This is . . . about it."*: Ibid.
29   *Their only . . . squash VisiOn.*: Ibid.
30   *Microsoft had . . . your hardware."*: Marlin Eller interview.
30   *"Bill would . . . they say."*: Scott McGregor interview, May 9,
      1997.
31   *"Bill was . . . other companies."*: Ibid.
34   *Procedures didn't exist.*: Marlin Eller interview.
39   *The beautiful . . . stage together.*: Microsoft press release, No-
      vember 10, 1983.
41   *"I just . . . Bill Gates."*: Rowland Hanson interview, November
      11, 1997.
42   *"You'd be . . . give you."*: Rowland Hanson E-mail, January 22,
      1998.
42   *$450,000.*: Rowland Hanson E-mail, January 17, 1998.
42   *April of 1984.*: *PC Magazine,* February 7, 1984.
43   *In Microsoft's . . . one week.*: Rowland Hanson E-mail, January
      21, 1998.

3. Be Like the Mac

45   *The company . . . of $1 billion.*: Microsoft bookshelf 1998.
45   *$75:Gates: How Microsoft's Mogul Reinvented an Industry and
      Made Himself the Richest Man in America,* by Stephen Manes
      and Paul Andrews, p. 184.
46   *To build . . . operating system.*: Marlin Eller interview.
46   *As part . . . Mac shipped.*: Ibid.
46   *Protecting the . . . both companies.*: Ibid.

46 *If the . . . with Apple.*: Ibid.

47 *"Why isn't . . . Mac even shipped.*: Scott McGregor interview, May 9, 1997.

47 *As per . . . was lifted.*: Marlin Eller interview.

47 *"a revolution in computing."*: *New York Times*, January 24, 1984.

47 *"Even if . . . to become."*: *Washington Post*, January, 30, 1984.

47 *Until that . . . at all.*: Steve Wood interview, August 22, 1995.

48 *The day . . . Windows developers.*: Marlin Eller interview.

48 *Furthermore, Gates . . . IBM PC?*: Neil Konzen interview, December 12, 1997.

48 *"How are . . . stuff together."*: Marlin Eller interview.

48 *Which is . . . system worked.*: Ibid.

49 *Change the . . . the Mac.*: Neil Konzen interview, December 12, 1997; and Scott McGregor interview, May 9, 1997.

49 *Gates simply . . . development process.*: Marlin Eller interview.

49 *"That's ridiculous . . . to OEMs."*: Ibid.

49 *Gates revered . . . Macintosh god.*: Marlin Eller interview; and Neil Konzen interview, December 12, 1997.

49 *Konzen was . . . the system.*: Ibid.

50 *"Good thing . . . no time!"*: Ibid.

51 *Almost all . . . least once.*: Marlin Eller interview; and Scott McGregor interview, May 5, 1997.

52 *Shortly after . . . at Microsoft.*: Marlin Eller interview.

53 *"Why would . . . it's fast."*: Ibid.

54 *"That's not . . . the Mac."*: Ibid.

55 *Instead, he . . . as overlapped.*: Ibid.

55 *At the . . . originally developed.*: Neil Konzen interview, December 12, 1997.

56 *"Cool, Neil's . . . system ready."*: Marlin Eller interview.

56 *"We aren't . . . it's pathetic."*: Steve Wood interview, August 22, 1995.

57 *Gates's preoccupation . . . development time.*: Marlin Eller interview.

4. Death March

59 *complaints in the press.*: *Computer Systems News*, October 22, 1984.

59 *Then, three . . . for months.*: Scott McGregor interview, May 5, 1997.

61 *"There was . . . own decisions."*: Steve Wood interview, August 22, 1995.

61 *Gates had . . . of code.*: Marlin Eller interview.

61 *Now, very . . . the competition.*: Steve Wood interview, August 22, 1995.

62 *"We'll make . . . stay here."*: Ibid.

63 *Ballmer's modus . . . should be.*: Scott McGregor interview, May 5, 1997.

63 *He and . . . McGregor aside.*: Marlin Eller interview; and Steve Wood interview, August 22, 1995.

65 *"The speed . . . to expect."*: Computer Systems News, October 22, 1984.

65 *"In light . . . better product."*: Ibid.

65 *Ballmer's designs . . . the papers.*: Marlin Eller interview.

65 *McGregor was . . . his office.*: Scott McGregor interview, May 5, 1997.

66 *Sadly, one . . . stock options.*: Ibid.

66 *"Nobody makes . . . this way."*: Marlin Eller interview.

66 *Ballmer obviously . . . let on.*: Ibid.

66 *"The energy . . . was great."*: Ibid.

67 *And Ballmer . . . a crisis.*: Ibid.

68 *Alexis Park Resort.*: Willamette Week, May 11–17, 1994.

68 *"To Dream the Impossible Dream."*: Ibid.

68 *"We just . . . time ago."*: Gates: How Microsoft's Mogul Reinvented an Industry and Made Himself the Richest Man in America, by Stephen Manes and Paul Andrews, p. 293.

68 *"The delay . . . it shipped."*: Willamette Week, May 11–17, 1994.

68 *"Running Windows . . . the Arctic."*: New York Times News Service/San Diego Union-Tribune, March 8, 1986.

69 *"Windows is . . . any alacrity."*: Ibid.

69 *"It seems . . . press Enter."*: Ibid.

5. Anything for IBM

72 *"I want . . . IBM deal."*: Steve Wood interview, August 22, 1995.

72 *"We all . . . it's over."*: Ibid.

72 *Wood, thinking . . . for him.*: Ibid.

73 *Microsoft didn't . . . program managers.*: Marlin Eller interview.

74 *Gates said . . . ever signed.*: New York Times, August 22, 1985.

78 *"No one . . . by this."*: Steve Wood interview, August 22, 1995.

79 *"By establishing . . . going through.":* San Jose Mercury News, June 14, 1987.
79 *"We had . . . kill Windows.":* Dave Weise interview, July 19, 1995.
80 *"Write for . . . be simple.":* Ibid.
81 *To make . . . each other.:* Marlin Eller interview.
81 *"Well, that's . . . the weekend.":* Steve Wood interview, August 22, 1995.
81 *Hursley itself . . . manicured grounds.:* Ibid.
82 *Strangely, the . . . debugging skills.:* Ibid.
84 *"We're not . . . ever managed.":* San Jose Mercury News, June 14, 1987.
85 *"This is . . . the 1990s.":* Wall Street Journal, October 31, 1988.
85 *"This is . . . all OS/2."* Rao Remala interview, August 22, 1995; and Dave Weise interview, July 19, 1995.

6. The Clandestine Effort

89 *In late . . . package deal.:* Murray Sargent interview, July 19, 1995.
89 *"Windows 286 . . . major transfusion.":* Ibid.
93 *At least . . . the market.:* Dave Weise interview, July 19, 1995.
93 *"The mind-set . . . IBM relationship.":* Ibid.
94 *"Microsoft would . . . the 1990s.":* National Review, January 24, 1994, p. 30.
94 *end developers' uncertainty.:* Ibid.

7. Bad Marriages End in Divorce

98 *Everyone close . . . haunt him.:* Dave Weise interview, July 19, 1995.
98 *"There is . . . and potency.":* New York Times, November 4, 1989.
99 *"Bill is . . . OS/2 100 percent.":* Dave Weise interview, July 19, 1995.
100 *Ironically, as . . . was strategic.:* Steve Wood interview, August 22, 1995.
100 *Until the . . . organizational chart.:* Lin Shaw interview, July 19, 1995.

101 *"Windows was . . . operating system."*: Ibid.
101 *"We're [the . . . projects successful."*: Dave Weise interview, July 19, 1995.
101 *In fact . . . Steve Wood.*: Marlin Eller interview.
101 *"OS/2 is . . . own thing."*: Steve Wood interview, August 22, 1995.
101 *Great Satan.*: Neil Konzen interview, December 12, 1997.
101 *Ballmer knew . . . get it.*: Steve Wood interview, August 22, 1995.
102 *He didn't . . . operating systems.*: Marlin Eller interview.
103 *As other . . . hire Cutler.*: Steve Wood interview, August 22, 1995; and Marlin Eller interview.
104 *Myhrvold had . . . Dave Patterson.*: Marlin Eller interview.
104 "Technology Shifts in the Operating Systems of the 1990s.": confidential Microsoft technical report written by Nathan Myhrvold, no date.
105 *"You cannot . . . so stupid."* Ibid., p. 12.
105 *"Price and . . . up front."*: Interoffice Microsoft memo, "Dreams of ModWin 2," written by Nathan Myhrvold, February 19, 1993, p. 12.
107 *"The divorce . . . our strategy."*: Steve Wood interview, August 22, 1995.
107 *"We lost . . . be successful."*: Dave Weise interview, July 19, 1995.
108 *The only . . . to Gates.*: Marlin Eller interview.

8. Pen Ultimate Warfare

113 *Established partly . . . called NewWave.*: Marlin Eller interview.
114 *"The relationship . . . an upgrade."*: "New Business Models for Wide Area Consumer Computing," interoffice memo written by Nathan Myhrvold, September 8, 1992, p. 2.
117 *Now it . . . the job.*: Marlin Eller interview.
118 *"I thought . . . we're wrong."*: *Startup: A Silicon Valley Adventure*, by Jerry Kaplan, p. 105.
118 *"All they . . . development team."*: Ibid.
120 *Kill GO Corp.*: Marlin Eller interview.
120 *Squashing the . . . of Microsoft.*: Ibid.
122 *The trip . . . at Microsoft.*: Ibid.
124 *Microsoft's lawyers . . . $1 million.*: Ibid.
124 *The lawyers counteroffered $100,000.*: Ibid.

125 *Microsoft gave . . . an "option.":* Ibid.
125 *"Xie Wei . . . for you.":* Ibid.
126 *"Ahh, I . . . about that.":* Ibid.

9. GO-ing Down

129 *"We'd rather . . . clear lies.":* Time, January 13, 1997, p. 56.
129 *Meanwhile, sitting . . . Wink Thorne.:* Marlin Eller interview.
129 *Playing it . . . in hand.:* Ibid.
130 *Then his . . . had promised.:* Ibid.
136 *Frink then . . . had shown.:* Ibid.
136 *"Microsoft had . . . infringement suit.":* Startup: A Silicon Valley Adventure, by Jerry Kaplan, p. 177.
137 *Microsoft's strategy . . . and IBM.:* Marlin Eller interview.
140 *So for . . . political relationships.:* Ibid.
141 *It was . . . more aware.:* Ibid.
141 *Gates said . . . making partner.:* Fortune, June 18, 1990, p. 82.
142 *"That's a . . . your blessings.":* Marlin Eller interview.

10. Meet the Jetsons

146 *Chez Gates . . . wood age.:* Marlin Eller interview.
146 *Originally, the . . . $60 million.:* Steve Wood interview, October 11, 1997.
146 *But there . . . new cement.:* Ibid.
148 *Gates initially . . . giant Matsushita.:* Greg Riker interview, April 30, 1997.
158 *By 1995 . . . new RV.:* Greg Riker interview, June 11, 1997.

11. High Road to Memphis—Low Road to MSN

161 *"It is . . . competitive threats.":* "Formats and Protocols for Consumer Information," interoffice memo written by Nathan Myhrvold, August 30, 1992.
162 *"New Business Models for Wide Area Consumer Computing,"* September 8, 1992, p. 2, and, *"Bootstrapping the On-line Information Business,"* October 12, 1992, both interoffice memos written by Nathan Myhrvold.

163   *"The people . . . similar phenomena."*: "Formats and Protocols for Consumer Information," Nathan Myhrvold interoffice memo, August 30, 1992, p. 1.

163   *Once a . . . software revenues.*: "New Business Models for Wide Area Consumer Computing," September 8, 1992, p. 9.

163   *"The goal . . . from Windows."*: "Bootstrapping the On-line Information Business," October 12, 1992, p. 11.

164   *"Market presence . . . some time."*: "New Business Models for Wide Area Consumer Computing," September 8, 1992, pp. 12–13.

164   *"Just roll . . . of you."*: Ibid., p. 13.

164   *"Our business . . . end users."*: "Bootstrapping the On-line Information Business," October 12, 1992, p. 5.

164   *"We cannot . . . that market."*: Ibid., p. 7.

175   *Torborg was . . . dangerous unknown.*: Marlin Eller interview.

12. Dodging Bullets

181   *The undocumented . . . operating systems.*: Lin Shaw interview, September 17, 1997.

182   *The fifth . . . of interest.*: *National Review*, January 24, 1994.

182   *The DoJ . . . hours.*: Court document—memo of U.S. in support of motion to enter final judgment, January 18, 1995.

182   *On May . . . national television.*: *Eye to Eye with Connie Chung*, CBS Burrelle's Information Services, May 19, 1994.

184   *On July . . . the wrist.*: Consent decree, July 14, 1994.

184   *In regard . . . "non-Microsoft product."*: Ibid.

186   *Sporkin said . . . "about me."*: United States Court of Appeals, court document no. 95-5037, decided June 16, 1995.

186   *At a . . . weren't true.*: Ibid.

187   *They claimed . . . other markets.*: Ibid.

187   *A 1987 . . . archrival Borland.*: *San Jose Mercury News*, February 22, 1995.

187   *"it is . . . is silent."*: United States Court of Appeals, court document no. 95-5037, decided June 16, 1995.

187   *"taking into . . . the decree."*: Ibid.

187   *Microsoft wanted . . . court judge.*: Ibid.

187   *"Microsoft, a . . . the marketplace."*: Ibid.

187   *On August . . . to another.*: Consent decree, August 21, 1995, final judgment.

13. Windows 95—Power in Numbers

189 *Two different plans.*: Lin Shaw interview, September 17, 1997.

191 *He told . . . never ship.*: Satoshi Nakajima interview, September 23, 1997.

193 *However, the . . . for help.*: London *Times*, August 8, 1996.

194 *"In order . . . should volunteer."*: Satoshi Nakajima interview, September 23, 1997.

195 *"To the . . . massively hosed."*: Chris Guzak interview, October 10, 1997.

196 *"I know . . . than once."*: Lin Shaw interview, July 19, 1995.

196 *In January . . . 95 bandwagon.*: Waggener Edstrom Web site.

200 *"Now I . . . perhaps free."*: Gates's "Internet Tidal Wave" memo, May 26, 1995.

200 *"A new . . . their products."*: Ibid.

200 *"I want . . . Windows asset."*: Ibid.

201 *"We need . . . browser preinstalled."* Ibid.

201 *"The Windows . . . Internet was."*: Lin Shaw interview, September 17, 1997.

202 *"Oh yeah . . . rewrote that."*: Chris Guzak interview, October 10, 1997.

202 *"A lot . . . from TCP/IP."*: Ibid.

202 *"Even by . . . comes later."*: Dave Weise interview, July 13, 1997.

203 *"We aren't . . . getting customers."*: Russ Siegelman, Microsoft confidential memo, July 12, 1995.

203 *$1 billion marketing campaign.*: Los Angeles *Times*, August 24, 1995.

204 *"I work . . . have it."*: USA Today, August 25, 1995.

204 *During the . . . spots ran.*: Waggener Edstrom Web site.

205 *In an . . . the market.*: Wall Street Journal, August 3, 1995.

205 *"I think . . . Windows 95."*: E-mail from Lin Shaw, September 4, 1997.

206 *"No, not . . . even close."*: Lin Shaw interview, September 17, 1997.

206 *"IE 1.0 . . . Plus Pack."*: Chris Guzak interview, October 10, 1997.

14. Continual Chaos

208 *"The Web . . . the Web."*: Chris Guzak interview, October 10, 1997.

208 *"Surprisingly it . . . the Internet."*: Satoshi Nakajima interview, September 23, 1997.

208 *"The Internet . . . past them."*: Steve Wood interview, August 22, 1995.

208 *"The Internet . . . the list]."*: Satoshi Nakajima interview, September 23, 1997.

209 *"There was . . . to us."*: Ibid.

209 *"We are . . . software division."*: *Seattle Post-Intelligencer*, December 8, 1995.

209 *"Blackbird" became "Internet Studio."*: Ibid.

210 *"If we . . . into NT."*: Steve Wood interview, October 11, 1997.

210 *"It made . . . shared code."*: Steve Wood interview, August 22, 1995.

210 *"When Windows . . . [software developers]."*: Chris Guzak interview, October 10, 1997.

210 *"It's been . . . that's true."*: Steve Wood interview, August 22, 1995.

211 *"Windows 98 . . . Windows 95."*: Lin Shaw interview, September 17, 1997.

211 *"Ultimately, investing . . . some point."*: Chris Guzak interview, October 10, 1997.

212 *"Microsoft doesn't . . . Windows 95."*: Steve Wood interview, October 11, 1997.

212 *At that . . . 74 percent.*: Zona Research, September 29, 1997.

212 *"I think . . . that point."*: Chris Guzak interview, October 10, 1997.

213 *"Frames probably . . . finished coding."*: Ibid.

213 *"We kind . . . time frame."*: Satoshi Nakajima interview, September 23, 1997.

214 *In April . . . team work.*: Lin Shaw interview, September 17, 1997.

214 *"NT 5.0 . . . on time."*: Chris Guzak interview, October 10, 1997.

214 *"Can you . . . at this?"*: Steve Wood interview, October 11, 1997.

215 *"I run . . . relaunch it."*: Ibid.

215 *"That was . . . good decision.":* Chris Guzak interview, October 10, 1997.

215 *"What I . . . first place.":* Steve Wood interview, October 11, 1997.

215 *"Gates' Greatest Power Grab.":* Fortune magazine, May 26, 1997.

216 *"NT 5.0 . . . bad way.":* Chris Guzak interview, October 10, 1997.

216 *"Fortunately if . . . that's scary.":* Ibid.

216 *"Microsoft's new . . . much power.":* Wall Street Journal, October 2, 1997.

217 *"Walt keeps . . . the desktop.":* Chris Guzak interview, October 10, 1997.

217 *"an abuse . . . to it.":* Wall Street Journal, October 21, 1997.

217 *"The threat . . . operating system.":* Department of Justice court document, October 20, 1997.

218 *"Microsoft is . . . multiple barrels.":* New York Times, December 17, 1997.

219 *"When they . . . doing so.":* Wall Street Journal, October 23, 1997.

219 *"Microsoft has . . . operating systems.":* Brad Chase affidavit, November 8, 1997.

219 *"The DoJ . . . Windows 95.":* Benjamin Slivka affidavit, December 2, 1997.

219 *"As a . . . Windows 95.":* Department of Justice court document, November 10, 1997.

220 *"To heck . . . Janet Reno.":* Reuters, October 22, 1997.

220 *"It's our . . . the functions.":* Wall Street Journal, October 23, 1997.

220 *"Our decision . . . operating system.":* Bill Gates shareholder transcript, November 1997.

220 *"witch hunt.":* Ibid.

221 *"Like the . . . Yes! Yes!":* Satoshi Nakajima interview, October 10, 1997.

221 *"It's a . . . you're doing.":* San Jose Mercury News, October 22, 1997.

221 *"Oh, there's . . . the salt.":* Ibid.

221 *"The big . . . Randy Johnson.":* New York Times, December 4, 1997.

221 *On December . . . preliminary injunction.:* Court document, December 11, 1997.

221 *"We see . . . the ruling.":* Wall Street Journal, December 12, 1997.

222 *"The court . . . doesn't boot.":* San Jose Mercury News, December 15, 1997.

222 *"In addition . . . a result.":* Court documents, Microsoft motion for expedited hearing, December 15, 1997.

222 *Three days . . . ship date.:* San Jose Mercury News, December 12, 1997.

222 *Microsoft went . . . Windows 95.:* Court documents, Microsoft motion for expedited hearing, December 15, 1997.

223 *"In the . . . our efforts.":* Wall Street Journal, December 23, 1997.

223 *Jody Powell.:* San Jose Mercury News, December 29, 1997.

224 *Newt Gingrich.:* Ibid.

224 *"Under court . . . federal judge.":* Microsoft press release, December 23, 1997.

225 *"Okay, this . . . a lawsuit.":* Microsoft home page/E-mail, July 29, 1997.

226 *"I don't . . . use them.":* San Jose Mercury News, January 8, 1998.

226 *"People view . . . overly sensitive.":* Ibid.

226 *"We need . . . the rhetoric.":* Associated Press, January 9, 1998.

226 *"Over the . . . that impression.":* Ibid.

228 *"We're naturally . . . this point.":* New York Times, January 15, 1998.

INDEX